HEALTH
FROM THE
HIVE

HEALTH
FROM THE
HIVE

Honey ...
Bee Pollen ...
Bee Propolis ...
Royal Jelly

CARLSON WADE

 KEATS PUBLISHING, INC., *New Canaan, Connecticut*

HEALTH FROM THE HIVE is not intended as medical advice. Its intent is solely informational and educational. Please consult a health professional should the need for one be indicated.

HEALTH FROM THE HIVE

Copyright © 1992 by Carlson Wade

All Rights Reserved

No part of this book may be reproduced in any form without the written consent of the publisher.

Library of Congress Cataloging-in-Publication Data
Wade, Carlson.
    Health from the hive / by Carlson Wade.
        p.   cm.
    Includes bibliographical references and index.
    ISBN 0-87983-581-8 : $9.95
    1. Bee products—Health aspects.   I. Title.
RA784.W237   1992
615'.321—dc20   92-21655
                                         CIP

Printed in the United States of America

Published by Keats Publishing, Inc.
27 Pine Street (Box 876)
New Canaan, Connecticut 06840-0876

To the honeybee ...
Sacred source of life

Contents

Introduction

The beehive—a fountain of youth and health!

Since the birth of the world, the honeybee has existed to create life for almost all other living creatures. Through the means of pollination, the honeybee has been able to nourish itself and all the inhabitants of the hive—unlike any other creature known. Life, as we know it, might not exist were it not for the miraculous honeybee, worshipped for its sacred abilities to fertilize plants and vegetation on our planet.

The honeybee is involved in preparing a set of foods that modern science recognizes as possessing amazing healing properties. Honey, pollen, propolis, and royal jelly are foods that are amazingly rich in a treasure of nutrients that doctors throughout the world have hailed as "natural medicines."

This book enters the beehive, joins with the swarms of buzzing bees to discover an astonishing civilization—right in the hive!

You will read the latest scientific reports on how these foods from the beehive can revitalize the body, reverse illness and roll back the aging clock; and you will learn the simple ways in which you can use these foods yourself to regenerate both body and mind.

In modern times, you need to protect your immune system. You are being assaulted by heavy metals in the air you breathe, with antibiotics and hormones in your meats, pesticides in your fruits and vegetables, herbicides in your grains and endless additives and preservatives in your foods.

Medical studies caution that we are facing an onslaught of never-before-seen organisms which threaten us daily.

How can you strengthen your immune system against these threats? Take a lesson from the honeybee. It has made itself and its residence, the hive, a fortress against environmental attack. That is how it has survived for over 45 million years!

The secret? A set of foods made in the hive. In this book I propose to show you how you can partake of these foods and boost your immune system to protect yourself against these toxic dangers of our chemical age.

CARLSON WADE

PART ONE

Honey

❖ The Worship of Honey— Healing Food from the Beehive

Since ancient times, honey has been considered of almost divine creation. Throughout antiquity right into our space age, honey and other foods from the beehive remain far and above anything else as having miracle healing powers.

At what stage in man's evolution was it recognized that honey has beneficial properties? We cannot know. Most likely, it was instinctive. Many lower animals go to great

3

distances to find the bee for its honey. While we know very little about the diet of early man, we do have evidence of honey forming a valuable part of the eating plan. Honey has always been more than a tasty, healing food. It has been a source of worship for its therapeutic powers.

❖ Honey in the Bible

We can discover much about the early use of honey from Biblical references. The use of honey as an internal and external remedial food must be much older than the history of medicine itself; it is, beyond doubt, the oldest panacea. In the most ancient scripts, we find references to honey as a glorified food, an ingredient of favored drinks, a popular natural medicine, and the principal component of liniments and plasters. The oldest mythologies praised the invigorating and health-giving qualities of honey. Many allusions were made to its magic healing powers. Honey is frequently mentioned and adored in the Bible.

> *My son, eat thou honey, because it is good; and the honeycomb, which is sweet to thy taste.*   PROVERBS 24:13

> *And I am come down to deliver them out of the hand of the Egyptians, and to bring them up out of that land unto a good land and a large, unto a land flowing with milk and honey.*   EXODUS 3:8

> *But Jonathan heard not when his father charged the people with the oath; wherefore he put forth the end of the*

4

rod that was in his hand, and dipped it in a honeycomb, and put his hand to his mouth; and his eyes were enlightened. Then said Jonathan, My father hath troubled the land; see, I pray you, how mine eyes have been enlightened, because I tasted a little of this honey.   I SAMUEL 14:27-29

Thou didst eat fine flour, and honey, and oil; and thou wast exceeding beautiful, and thou didst prosper into a kingdom.   EZEKIEL 16:13

"Hast thou found honey? Eat so much as is sufficient for thee."   PROVERBS 25:16

He made him ride on the high places of the earth, that he might eat the increase of the field; and he made him to suck honey out of the rock.   DEUTERONOMY 32:13

He should have fed them also with the finest of the wheat; and with honey out of the rock should I have satisfied thee. [In the countryside bees would frequently build nests in the side of cliffs and rocks.]   PSALM 81:16

And after a time he returned to take her, and he turned aside to see the carcass of the lion; and behold, there was a swarm of bees and honey in the carcass of the lion. And he took thereof in his hands, and went on eating, and came to his father and mother, and he gave them, and they did eat; but he told them not that he had taken the honey out of the carcass of the lion.   JUDGES 14: 8-9.

We came unto the land whither thou sentest us, and surely it floweth with milk and honey; and this is the fruit of it.   NUMBERS 13:27

> *More to be desired are they (the judgment of the Lord) than gold, yea, than much fine gold: sweeter also than honey and the honeycomb.* PSALM 19:10

> *What is sweeter than honey? and what is stronger than a lion?* JUDGES 14:18

So we see that honey was prized as a source of sustenance, so much that the Israelites would never make sacrifices using honey, which they considered to be of special value and healing.

❖ Honey in Ancient Egypt

During the 40th century B.C., honey was used in most households as a sweetener. The Egyptians valued honey highly; it was commonly used as a tribute or payment. It was also used to feed sacred animals.

In the Fifth Dynasty temple of Niweserre at Abusir, built around 2500 B.C., there are scenes depicting early beekeeping. The hives appear as cylindrical pipes piled up in horizontal rows. Each hollow tube, made of sun-baked mud, appears to be about four feet in length and about eight inches in diameter. The pipes are situated together in a manner to be protected from the sun's heat by a mud coating; in some cases, shade is provided by tree branches. In many parts of the Middle East, similar hives can still be seen.

Honey was used as part of the Egyptian diet. In the tomb of Rekhara of the Eighteenth Dynasty, built around

1500 B.C., there are drawings showing men baking cakes with honey. From surviving records, Rameses III presented a foreign king with a gift of 7050 jars of honey.

Egyptians chiseled a likeness of the honeybee on many monuments, painted scenes of beekeepers tending bees on the walls of their tombs and even recorded activities of this hard-working creature in holy hieroglyphics inscribed on papyrus scrolls. Writings over 2000 years old reveal that Egyptian physicians called honey the "universal healer." During this time, Egyptians paid three drachmas per quart for strained honey.

Next to hieroglyphic representations, the wall paintings of the royal tombs demonstrate the great national importance of honey. In most tombs, bees and honey are represented pictorially. Honeycombs, honey cakes, sealed jars of honey and lotus blossoms were placed next to the sarcophagi as food for the souls of the dead.

In the tomb of Pa-Ba-Sa, in Thebes, the entire wall is decorated by rows of bees. A man is shown pouring honey into a pail, another is kneeling and praying before a pyramid of honeycombs. On the wall of the tomb of Rekh-Mi-Re all phases of the honey industry are depicted: how the combs were removed from the hives with the aid of smoke, the baking of honey cakes, the filling and sealing of jars, etc.

The Egyptian papyri, representing the oldest civilization in the world, often refer to honey, especially to its medicinal value. Almost all Egyptian medicines contained honey, wine and milk. Honey sacrifices were offered to the deities. The frequent symbolic use of bees in Egypt must be attributed not only to the fact that honey was an important article of commerce and a valuable food and medicinal substance but to the admiration of the Egyptians for the diligence, industry, order, economy, endurance, intelligence and courage of the bees and their loyalty to a sovereign. The bees are the only creatures which are entirely subjugated to a ruler. Next to the signatures of Egyptian kings could be seen the figure of a bee.

The ancient Egyptians were habitual beer drinkers. The land was ill-suited to the cultivation of the grape vine. Xenophon (400 B.C.) mentions an Egyptian beverage made of wheat, barley and honey.

❖ Honey in Greece

Honey appears in much of Greek mythology. For example, the Greeks credit Aristaeus, son of Apollo and Cyrene, with bringing the knowledge of bees and honey to mortal man. That is, Aristaeus was educated by the Muses, the nine Greek goddesses who were patrons of the arts. This relationship led to bees being called the "birds of the Muses." It was also believed that if a bee touched a child's lips, he would develop magical qualities to perform the various arts. Legend says that bees kissed such philosophers as Sophocles and Plato.

Ambrosia, the food, and nectar, the drink of the gods, were made of honey. The honey of Mt. Hymettus was a daily food of Athens. The mountain was covered with fragrant wild flowers, basically thyme; the air was scented with the delightful fragrance of the blooms. Bees were partial to these hills. Ancient Attica, with its area of forty square miles, recorded twenty thousand hives during the time of Pericles (429 B.C.). All ancient Greek authors praised the medicinal and nutritional value of Attica honey, "the crowning dish of all feasts." The oldest ruins in the rural districts of Greece are buildings which originally housed the hives. These stone edifices were built high, to outwit the cunning of the bears, arch-enemies of bees and connoisseurs of honey. An ancient custom was the offering of honey to the gods and to spirits of the dead. Mead, an alcoholic drink made with honey, was considered the drink of the Greek gods.

❖ Honey in Rome

In Roman times, honey served as a food preservative as well as being part of the regular fare. According to Coelius Apicius, author of *The Roman Cookery Book*, each villa had a separate enclosure reserved for beehives, tended by a servant. This enclosure known as a *mellarius*, would provide a daily supply of honey. The Roman author Virgil (70–19 B.C.) in his *Georgics* or *Art of Husbandry* devotes a big section to the art of beekeeping. Virgil tells how honey is harvested and used and tells how it may improve the quality of poor wine thus:

> *You'll strain sweet honey, sweet and clear enough*
> *To tame the bitter flavor of the wine.*

Virgil also says, "Next I sing of honey, the heavenly

ethereal gift." He then praises honey in the *Aeneid* as "the sweet-scented honey, fragrant with thyme."

Pliny the Elder, who lived in Rome between 23 and 79 A.D. and wrote the great *Natural History*, believed that the daily use of honey would insure a long and healthy life. He tells how foods and drinks, mixed with honey, were seen in the daily menus of Rome. It was a courteous act of the Romans to offer a respected guest some honey, fresh from the hives. The host welcomed his visitors with the greeting, "Here is honey which the gods provided for your health."

Pliny also tells of other lands, including the British Isles, in which honey was considered a rich treasure of health.

So we see that since the dawn of time honey has been prized. It was enjoyed throughout Europe, and conquering Spaniards found that the natives of 16th-century Mexico and Central America had also developed beekeeping. A distinct family of honeybees were native to the Americas.

European settlers introduced European honeybees to New England in about 1638. The North American natives called these honeybees the "white man's flies."

❖ What Is Honey?

It is a sweet, viscous fluid produced by bees from plant nectar. It is a golden sweet elixir concocted by the honeybees. No one has been able to devise a way to manufacture this delicious golden liquid. It is the result of the cooperative efforts of every bee that lives and works in the murmurous hive, abuzz with constant activity.

❖ The Bee Colony

The bee colony is a thriving home for as many as 50,000 members, sometimes even more.

The modern hive is a series of boxes, stacked atop one another, as opposed to a hollow tree. Inside these boxes hang frames in which the bees build their combs; the bottom set of boxes is the actual working and living area for the colony of bees. All the boxes stacked above are called "supers" and are placed there by the beekeeper for the bees to fill with honey.

Three types of bees live in the colony:

Queen: This bee lives for two or three years and exists primarily to produce eggs. She mates only once and is capable of laying 1500 eggs every day until her death. When necessary (usually at the beginning of Spring) the queen bee lays unfertilized eggs which produce drones.

Drones: These bees have only one purpose in life, to mate with a new queen. They do not work in the hive, and do not gather pollen or nectar. When food supplies get low or the other bees are too busy to care for them, they are pushed out of the hive to die.

Workers: These bees are the most interesting. Not more than one day after the worker emerges from her brood cell, she begins her life of unending toil. The worker has these duties:

1. To clean the brood cells in preparation for the queen's egg-laying process and feed the larvae from the royal jelly she secretes. (It takes over 3000 workers over 10 hours of nursing and feeding for a single larva to emerge as a healthy contributor to hive life.) When the worker bee is about two weeks old, her nursing duties end and she becomes a "house bee."

2. As "house bee," she is responsible for the inside of the hives; she produces wax and repairs combs, helps unload nectar, pollen, water and propolis (a sticky substance used in hive building) which are then delivered by older bees to the hive. She is then responsible for storing food and distributing it to the brood, cleaning the hive of dead bees, and protecting the hive from invaders. If it gets too hot, she fans the hive; if it gets really hot, she flies out, gets water (in her honey stomach) and bathes the entire hive. After her days of tending house are completed, she becomes a field bee. Her life lasts only five weeks.

❖ Honeybee Facts at a Glance

The Colony: Honeybees are social insects, with a marked division of labor between the various types of bees in the hive. A hive of honeybees includes a queen, drones and workers.

The Queen: The only sexually developed female in the hive, she is larger than either the drone or the worker bee. If a two-day-old larva is selected by the workers to be reared as a queen, she will emerge from her cell eleven days later to mate in flight with approximately 18 drone (male) bees. During this mating, she receives several million sperm cells, which last her entire lifespan of nearly two years. The queen starts to lay eggs about two days after mating. A very productive queen can lay 3,000 eggs in a single day.

The Drones: Drones are much stouter than queens or workers. The drone is a male and has no stinger. He does not collect food or pollen from flowers, nor does he secrete wax. His sole purpose is to mate with the queen. If the colony is short on food, drones are often kicked out of the hive.

The Workers: Workers, the smallest bees in the colony, are sexually undeveloped females. A colony can have 50,000 to 60,000 workers. The lifespan of a worker bee varies according to the time of the year. It is approximately 28 to 35 days. Workers that are reared in September and October, however, can live throughout the winter. Workers feed the queen and larvae, collect nectar, guard the hive entrance and help keep the hive cool by fanning their wings.

In addition, honeybees produce the wax comb. The comb is composed of hexagonal cells which have walls that are only 2/1000 of an inch thick, but support 25 times their own weight.

The honeybee's wings stroke 11,400 times per minute, thus making their distinctive buzz.

❖ How Honey Is Produced

The bee gathers the nectar from the flower; the liquid passes into its honey sac and is mixed with acid secretions at the base of its tongue. The bee then flies back to the hive where the honey is deposited. A brewing process takes place at a temperature of 80 to 85° F. (In the very heart of the hive, it may be 97° F.) The bee is not a natural honey maker; the younger ones are taught by the more experienced ones.

Bees will fly two to three miles to find flowers with the right nectar. A bee might travel as much as 40,000 miles to produce honey to fill a single one-pound jar.

After the honey has been produced by the bee, the beekeeper uncaps the combs, placing them in a centrifugal force machine (extraction) to remove the honey. It is then delivered to the plant where it is simply strained and heated in order to liquefy it so it can be poured into the jar.

The average yield of honey per hive is 45 pounds. Approximately 200 million pounds of honey are produced yearly in the United States and an equivalent amount in the rest of the world.

❖ Honey, It's a Natural

Honey adds beautiful golden color and delightful sweet flavor to bring out the best in so many foods. It is available in a variety of forms.

Liquid honey, which is free of visible crystals, is extracted from the comb in the hive by centrifugal force, gravity, straining or other means. It is especially convenient for cooking, but can be used as a spread as well. Most honey in the United States is sold in liquid form.

Creme or spun honey is finely crystallized. While all honey will crystallize in time, the crystallization of creme honey is controlled so that at room temperature it can be spread like butter on toast, biscuits, muffins, combined with other foods for sandwiches; or even be used as a cake filling. Outside the U.S., creme or spun honey is the preferred form.

Comb honey is sold with the honey contained in the cells of the honeybee's wax comb in which it was produced. The comb is edible.

Cut comb refers to honey which has chunks of comb honey in the jars.

❖ Caring for Honey

Honey should be stored at room temperature. All forms of honey, including liquid honey, will crystallize naturally over a period of time. The crystals can be dissolved by placing the jar in warm water, or by microwave cooking one cup of honey in a microwave-safe container on HIGH for two to three minutes—stirring every 30 seconds.

15

❖ Honey Color and Flavor— It All Depends on Where the Bees Buzz

Honey has different flavors and colors, depending on the location and kinds of flowers. Climatic conditions of the area also influence its flavor and color. Specifically, the color and flavor of honeys differ, depending on the nectar source (the blossoms) visited by the honeybees. The color ranges from nearly colorless to dark brown. The flavor varies from delectably mild to distinctively bold, depending on where the honeybees buzzed.

There are more than 300 unique types of honey available, each originating from a different floral source. As a general rule, the light-colored honey is milder. The dark-colored honey is stronger.

Honey is produced in every state, but depending on location of floral source, certain types of honey are produced in only a few regions. Honey is also produced in most countries around the world.

Here is a look at some of the most common honeys and their floral sources:

Acacia honey is a pale yellow honey with an exquisite, delicate taste. China is the major source for acacia honey. It is being increasingly produced in California.

Alfalfa honey, produced extensively throughout the United States and Canada, is light in color with a pleasingly mild flavor and aroma.

Basswood honey is characterized by its distinctive "biting" flavor. It is generally water-white in color and strong in flavor.

Buckwheat honey is a dark, full-bodied honey. It is produced in Minnesota, New York, Ohio, Pennsylvania and Wisconsin as well as in eastern Canada.

Clover honey has a pleasing, mild taste. Clovers have contributed more to honey production in the United States than any other group of plants. White clover, Alsike clover and the white and yellow sweet clovers are most important for honey production. Depending on the location and type of source clover, this type of honey varies in color from water-white to light amber to amber.

Eucalyptus honey comes from one of the larger plant genera, containing over 500 distinct species and many hybrids. As may be expected with a diverse group of plants, eucalyptus honey varies greatly in color and flavor but tends to be a stronger flavored honey. Eucalyptus is the major source of honey in Australia.

Fireweed honey is light in color and comes from a perennial herb that affords wonderful bee pastures in the northern and Pacific states and Canada. Fireweed grows in the open woods, reaching a height of three to five feet with spikes of attractive pinkish flowers.

Orange blossom honey, often a combination of citrus sources, is usually light in color and mild in flavor with a fresh scent and light taste reminiscent of the blossom. It is produced in Florida, southern California and southern Texas.

Sourwood honey's source is a small to medium-size tree common in the southern part of the Appalachian mountains from West Virginia and southern Pennsylvania to northern Georgia. The honey is light in color and heavy-bodied with a fine mild flavor.

Tulip poplar or tulip tree honey is dark amber in color. The flavor is not as strong as you would expect of a dark honey. It is produced from southern New England west to southern Michigan and south to the Gulf states east of the Mississippi.

Tupelo honey is a premium honey produced in the southeastern United States. It is heavy-bodied and high in levulose (fruit sugar). It is usually light in color with a mild, distinctive taste.

Remember, there are more than 300 types of honey available, not to mention different blends and combinations so you can enjoy a different honey every day of the year!

❖ How to Use Honey

As a natural sweetener, in baking, over fruits, in cereals, as an ingredient in cooking, etc.

Substituting Honey for Sugar in Baking.

Basically, select a strongly flavored honey for spreads and other recipes where a distinct flavor is desired. Select mildly flavored honeys for use when delicate flavors prevail.

When baking, honey retains moisture. It is twice as sweet as sugar; therefore, you use half as much to reach the same level of sweetness. Since there are 39 calories in one tablespoon of sugar, and 63 calories in one tablespoon of honey, your intake of calories is actually less when using honey.

Substitute honey for sugar, by reducing the liquid called for by ½ cup for every cup of honey used to replace the sugar. Add ½ teaspoon salt-free or reduced salt baking soda to the recipe for every cup of honey substituted. Bake at a temperature 25 degrees lower than that called for in the recipe. In cookie recipes using eggs and no additional liquid, increase the flour by approximately 2 tablespoons per cup of honey or enough flour to give the desired consistency (a stiff dough in the case of cookies). Chill before shaping and baking.

❖ Honey Nutrition Facts

Honey is twice as sweet as table sugar, therefore 50 percent less can be used to sweeten foods, resulting in a lower caloric value when honey is substituted for sugar on a per weight basis.

Honey is the only natural sweetener known that needs no additional refining or processing to be utilized. Its unique flavors derive from more than 300 floral sources.

Honey is an invert sugar composed of 38 percent fructose, 31 percent glucose, 1 percent sucrose and 9 percent other sugars along with water, and various amounts of vitamins and minerals.

As a carbohydrate, honey is a good supplier of energy at 63 calories per tablespoon. Honey contains beneficial amounts of riboflavin, thiamine and ascorbic acid and varying amounts of minerals.

Because of honey's unique composition, it is digested a little differently than other sweeteners. When compared to table sugar, honey has less of an effect on blood glucose and insulin levels due to its higher fructose content.

❖ Honey Is a Source of Youthful Energy

Looking for more energy? Honey can give you a youthful boost. Here are reports on this rejuvenating food from the hive:

• Athletes in many countries have found that honey gives them more energy and staying power. Honey is a balanced mixture of glucose, fructose and nutrients produced by bees that provides energy to be rapidly assimilated into the bloodstream without any pre-routing during the complicated process of digestion.

• The glycogen in a spoonful of honey is said to pass into the bloodstream in 10 minutes to produce quick energy. If taken with a calcium supplement, the glucose in honey can increase the body's uptake of the mineral by nearly 25 percent, according to the U.S. Department of Agriculture nutritionist Richard J. Wood. "Our findings indicate that glucose could be an effective way of enhancing intestinal absorption of calcium."

• Glucose boosts the absorption of such essential minerals as zinc and magnesium, unlike sugar which, according to kinesiology researchers at the University of California at Los Angeles, can weaken bone strength and block growth by inhibiting calcium absorption in the intestines and reducing the amount that gets to bones.

◆ Unlike sugar, honey has none of sugar's potential as a possible carcinogen, says Stephen Seely of the University of Manchester in England and Dr. D. F. Horrobin of Nova Scotia, who investigated the amount of sugar eaten in 20 countries and compared figures with the incidence of breast cancer in those countries. Results? The countries with the most breast cancer had the highest consumption of sugar: the United States, England, the Netherlands, Ireland, Canada and Denmark. The countries with the least breast cancer had the least consumption of sugar: Italy, Yugoslavia, Spain, Portugal and Japan. Sugar causes insulin to be over-secreted by the pancreas and poured into the bloodstream. This reaction acts on certain tissues known as low-priority to become a mild carcinogen (cancer-causer.) The human breast is an organ of low priority.

In Japan, the average consumption of sugar and sugary foods is only 60 grams a day or 15 teaspoons. In the U.S., the average American consumes 36 teaspoons of sugar every day![1]

❖ Honey Heals Wounds

In one medical study, 58 people with wounds that resisted antibiotics for more than two years experienced dramatic healing after one week of topical application of honey. The researchers believe it may be honey's acidity or drying power or a bacteria-killing ingredient called *inhibine* that allowed the sores to finally heal.[2]

In another report, Richard D. Heimbach, M.D., a wound-healing expert and researcher at Methodist Hospital in San Antonio, Texas, tells us, "Antibiotics will help a wound heal only if it is non-healing due to infection. But infection might not be the only problem in a wound. In such cases, honey seems to be able to attack wounds in other ways besides fighting infection.[3]

How to Use Honey for Healing.

You might try a bit of honey on a small cut or sore and cover with a bandage. Do NOT put honey on a burn since burns become infected too easily. Be sure to consult your health practitioner if you see signs of infection: swelling, excessive redness and heat. No topical remedy will help if sores arise from chronic disease, such as poor circulation from diabetes. For topical use, select only fresh, processed honey. Raw honey or honey that's been crystallizing in your pantry for ages may have some resistant bacteria.

❖ Using Honey as a Natural Medicine

Dr. Alfred Vogel, famed Swiss healer who has helped thousands of patients at his clinic with the use of natural remedies, author of *The Nature Doctor*, has this to tell us about honey:

Our interest lies in the remedial value of honey, which has earned a high mark for itself in natural medicine. In the ancient world, honey was well known and appreciated for its healing properties, but as time went on that knowledge fell into oblivion. The rediscovery and scientific explanation of the value of honey, however, has enabled it once more to assume its rightful place among natural remedies.

There is no doubt that honey and its medicinal value were known as far back as Biblical times, as it is mentioned in a number of ancient records. Honey is the best form of carbohydrate and is easily absorbed by the body.

What is more, experience has shown that honey increases the medicinal effect of natural remedies that are good for the respiratory organs. If you want to take advantage of this fact, simply add the indicated number of drops of a given remedy to a teaspoon of honey or to warm water sweetened with honey. Sipping this honey water together with the remedies will enhance their effect; for example, in cases of catarrh or disorders of the bronchial tubes or lungs, the prescribed medicines will have a much faster and stronger effect if taken with honey. It is for this reason that the pine bud syrup Santasapina contains honey.

Honey Salve—a Healer.

Dr. Vogel suggests:

Mix a teaspoon of honey with 20-30 drops of Echinaforce tincture and you will have a splendid healing salve for grazes, minor wounds and cuts, boils, and even scabs and crusts.

For wounds that refuse to heal properly, mix some honey with 10 percent horseradish; the horseradish can be finely grated, or use the fresh juice or tincture. Apply this reliable natural remedy to the affected part, and you will be surprised at the good result. This mixture is an excellent remedy for whitlows, nail mold and similar stubborn conditions that suppurate (form pus) and take a long time to heal.

Treating Arthritis and Gout with Honey Packs.

Dr. Vogel suggests that for these conditions

You will find the external application of honey a great relief. Add one teaspoon of comfrey tincture or Symphosan to four tablespoons of honey, mix thoroughly in a cup, then heat the mixture in a double saucepan.

Fold a cloth three or four times, soak it in the hot honey mixture and apply to the parts where the pain is worst— the hands, elbows, knees and feet. This treatment is best given in the evening, so you can leave the pack on overnight. In order to retain the heat for longer, place on top of the pack a bag of cherry stones that have been heated on the stove; a bag of hot hay flowers or camomile will serve the same purpose. Then wrap a warm cloth around everything.

. . . Some patients have been helped by this treatment to the extent that they were once again able to walk or move their hands without feeling any pain.

It is worthwhile repeating these honey packs for several weeks until you find relief. If you do not have any herbs at

*your disposal, honey packs can be made without them. The
effect will still be very beneficial, even though it might take
longer.*[4]

Helps Improve Basic Health.

Paavo Airola, N.D., author of *How to Get Well*, offers a
thumbnail benefit of honey.

*Honey possesses miraculous nutritional and medicinal prop-
erties and has been used for healing purposes since early
history. It has been found that most centenarians in Russia
and Bulgaria use honey liberally in their diets.*

*Better than any other food, honey fulfills Hippocrates'
requirement for an ideal food: Our food should be our medicine—our medicine should be our food. Honey increases
calcium retention in the system, prevents nutritional anemia,
is beneficial in kidney and liver disorders, colds, poor circulation and complexion problems.*

Dr. Airola says that natural honey is the only sweetener
used in his highly acclaimed Airola Diet, but, he warns,
"use it sparingly—only one or two tablespoons a day—
particularly in the diet of older people.[5]

❖ Long Live The Bee

The U.S. Department of Agriculture estimates that about 3.5
million U.S. acres of fruits, vegetables, oil seeds and legume

seed crops depend on insect pollination. Another 63 million acres derive some benefit from insect pollination.

About 80 percent of insect crop pollination is accomplished by honeybees. Approximately one-third of the total human diet is derived directly or indirectly from insect-pollinated plants (fruits, legumes and vegetables.)

Alone in the animal kingdom, only the bee has vital work to do. Without her ability to carry the pollen that fertilizes the plants and flowers, many species would fail to survive. The bee improves the environment and enriches her corner of the world with her presence.

Ecologists reckon that over 100,000 species of plants would die out and become extinct without the pollinating work of the bee. Without these plants, life as we know it (perhaps all life) would become extinct.

❖ About Bee Stings

Bees will live and let live. But you need to obey certain rules to avoid bee stings. Bees have an unusually sharp sense of smell and dislike certain odors, such as perspiration, tobacco and alcohol. An onion breath is unforgivable. Bees will attack an offender who wears perfume, scented rouge, or lipstick.

A bee will sting to defend itself, so approach a hive with care. Sharp colors will also arouse the bee, so it is best to wear neutral colors. If you look and smell like a flower, the bee will try to get pollen out of you via a sting!

Incidentally, once a bee stings, it soon dies, because in the process of stinging it loses not only the barb, but its sheath and encasing muscles. To avoid depleting the bee population, avoid giving bees reasons for stinging you.

If you go near a hive, here are some simple rules:

1) Walk and move quietly, slowly and gently.

2) Visit the hive between 10:00 A.M. and 2:00 P.M., when the greatest numbers of the worker bees are out in the fields.

3) Choose a bright, sunny day. Bees are often in an ill humor on cool, wet or overcast days; they do not fly in large numbers foraging for nectar but frequently milk near the hive.

4) Never make a slapping motion at a bee flying near you. This gesture infuriates bees. The offended bee you have threatened may let out a yell of anger that may bring hundreds of other bees to her defense.

5) Make sure your clothes (and yourself) are free of odors of any kind.

6) Avoid breathing on the bees when you bend over the hive, since the slightest odor may disturb them.

7) Take care not to pinch or injure a bee while manipulating the hive. The entire colony may think it necessary to rescue her and drive you away.

8) Remain calm. Your presence is then less likely to disturb the bees. No talking in the presence of bees, lest you are considered an enemy!

❖ Honey Trivia

♦ Honey bees must tap two million flowers to make one pound of honey.

* A hive of bees must fly over 55,000 miles to bring you one pound of honey.
* The average worker honeybee makes only 1/12 teaspoon of honey in her lifetime.
* The honeybee flies about 15 miles per hour.
* It takes one ounce of honey to fuel a bee's flight around the world.
* The honeybee has five eyes.
* Mead is a form of honey wine. It is believed to have been made from the honeycombs which would be immersed in water and left to ferment.
* Bees have been producing honey from flowering plants for 10 to 20 million years.
* Drambuie is a Scotch liqueur made with honey.
* Each honeycomb cell has exactly six sides—never any more or less!
* Modern science says it is aerodynamically impossible for a honeybee to fly, that her fragile gossamer wings cannot lift her heavy ungainly body into the air and sustain flight. But the bee does not know this—and she flies! The bee has not changed one bit since the moment of her creation.
* Each person in the United States consumes about 1.1 pounds of honey per year.
* The Church of Jesus Christ of Latter-Day Saints (the Mormons) holds the honeybee in very high regard. The name *Deseret*, a term from their Book of Mormon, signifies industry, insofar as the honeybee is concerned. A beehive appears on the Great Seal of Utah, which is known as the beehive state. Many Mormon industries are honored by the name Deseret, the term for honeybee.
* The honeybee has four wings.

- There are an estimated 211,600 beekeepers in the United States. There are an estimated 3.2 million colonies of bees.
- A honeybee visits up to 100 flowers during one collection trip.
- Honeybees can communicate with one another. "Dancing" honeybees do a dance which alerts other bees where nectar and pollen is located. The dance explains direction and distance. Bees also communicate with pheromones (scents).
- Cupid, the Roman god of romance and love, dipped his arrows in honey.
- The word "super" refers to the hive box of the beekeeper in which honey is stored.

The honeybee is environmentally friendly. Bees do not pollute the environment. They do not require special land use. They are a vital part in the reproduction of plant life since a majority of all plants on our planet would not exist if they were not pollinated by bees.

Bee products are cruelty-free. Although hives are "robbed" of some of their bounty, this is never done at the expense of the bee; that would be similar to killing the proverbial goose that lays the golden egg. Man has learned to "farm" bees. And bee products need not be tested experimentally on other animals since they are food products.

With this awareness, you can appreciate why the honeybee has long been worshipped. It may well be the very source of life!

PART TWO

Bee Pollen

❖ Food of the Gods—for Mortals

The ancients called it "the life-giving dust" and "ambrosia"—the grains of flower pollen together with honey that could revitalize wellbeing. It seemed the gods themselves would feed on it.

❖ What Is This Power Food?

Bee pollen is the ultrafine powder that makes up the male element of a flower. Bees gather this pollen in microscopic amounts and bring it into the hive for food.

By instinct, bees collect only the most nutritive and healthy pollens. They will bypass poor pollen. As the bees bring the pollen into the hive, some of it falls off their legs onto the bottom of the enclosure. It is this pollen which is recognized as an amazing source of potent vitamins, minerals, amino acids and other ingredients that promote healing of many ailments as well as longevity.

After the bees collect and deposit pollen in the hive, they improve it by adding a small portion of nectar to it. This shapes the pollen into manageable, tiny granules and encloses them in a form that shields them from outside assault and transforms them into a pure, all-natural and highly potent life-giving, life-extending food.

In brief, as the industrious honeybee climbs onto the petals in search of nectar, she brushes past the pollen bearing stamen and collects the golden grain in tiny baskets at the back of her legs to feed the occupants of the hive.

❖ Pollen: What's in It for You?

As we have seen, pollen is the male element of the flower. When examined under the microscope, it is seen as a very fine powder, an infinite amount of grains of different forms and designs representing the specific flower from which it comes.

This fine powder, containing richly concentrated nutritive and healing properties, forms the ovules, the starting point of the production of fruits, grains, legumes and vegetables.

Basically, pollen gathered by the bees is mixed with nectar to make it more solid and of a particular consistency to form the pellets, the form that is carried into the hive.

A bee brings two loads of pollen at a time in her pollen baskets; that is, two pellets which weigh an average of 20 milligrams (one milligram is one thousandth of a gram; one ounce has 30 grams). It takes a bee approximately one hour to collect an amount that adds up to about four million pollen grains.

Therefore, one teaspoon (the customary recommended dose) contains about 1200 pellets; or about 2.5 billion grains of pollen—each of which has all the potency to fertilize and create a fruit, a grain and so forth.

Yes, there is power in pollen.

But what is in it for you?

The composition of pollen, like that of honey and royal jelly, is extremely complex. An analysis shows a very richly concentrated amount of nitrogenous materials known as protein, minerals, amino acids along with a treasure of other non-isolated and different trace elements.

❖ Looking into the Power-Packed Pollen Pellet

To begin with, let us look at the most abundant and valuable components found in this power-packed pellet— namely, amino acids, the stuff of which protein is made.

35

Proteins are found in meat, fish, eggs, dairy products, beans, nuts and seeds. As nitrogenous substances, they vary in potency, according to the source. Protein content may be 7%, 30% or even 50%, depending upon the product. But at the same time, animal protein foods contain saturated fat, cholesterol and other substances that may be detrimental to your health if taken to excess. Therefore, it makes sense to include a meatless source of protein in your diet.

In some tests, after the lipids (fats) were removed, pollen had about 30% protein. In a typical pollen product, the amino acids appear in this potency for an average serving:

Cystine	0.6 grams
Histidine	1.5 grams
*Tryptophan	1.6 grams
*Methionine	1.7 grams
*Phenylalanine	3.5 grams
*Threonine	4.6 grams
Arginine	4.7 grams
*Isoleucine	4.7 grams
*Leucine	5.6 grams
*Lysine	5.7 grams
*Valine	6.0 grams
Glutamic acid	9.1 grams

From the preceding, we see that pollen contains those amino acids most valuable for your body, since your system is unable to manufacture them (indicated by *). Furthermore, these amino acids come from natural sources and are power-packed.

The bees instinctively know and select pollens rich in nitrogenous matter and avoid the poor ones!

❖ Vitamins in Pollen

Although products do vary in potency, generally speaking, one gram of raw pollen will have the following:

Vitamin B1 (thiamine)	9.2 milligrams
Vitamin B2 (riboflavin)	18.5 milligrams
Vitamin B6 (pyridoxine)	5 milligrams
Niacin	200 milligrams
Pantothenic acid	30 to 50 milligrams

Other Vitamins:

The content of vitamin C varies from 7 to 15 milligrams. One gram of pollen also has about 10 milligrams of beta-carotene, a precursor of vitamin A, appreciable traces of vitamin E (tocopherol), and about 3.4 to 6.8 milligrams of folic acid.

What About Sugar?

By its very nature, pollen has a certain amount of glucosides but bees add a little nectar to agglutinate the grains; that is, to give them sufficient adherence to form the pellets.

37

Bee pollen has from 10% to 15% sugars, mainly in the form of fructose and glucose.

What About Its Color?

The color of pollen varies according to its source; it may be creamy white to very dark. Pollen contains a variety of pigments, some of which have been isolated. Buy the pollen according to its potency, not necessarily its color.

❖ Protein in Meat Vs. Pollen

You are looking at a superb package of protein when you see yourself in a mirror. All that shows—muscles, skin, hair, nails, eyes—are protein tissues. Teeth contain a little protein. Most of what you do not see is protein, too—blood and lymph, heart and lungs, tendons and ligaments, brain and nerves and all the rest of you. Genes, those mysterious controllers of heredity, are a particular kind of protein. Hormones, the chemical regulators of body processes, and enzymes, the sparkplugs of chemical reactions, also are proteins.

Proteins are unique in that they contain the element nitrogen. All our foodstuffs—fats, starches, sugars and proteins—contain the elements carbon, hydrogen and oxygen in varying proportions. Because proteins contain them and also nitrogen, they have a special importance and power.

Where Do Proteins Come From?

Proteins have to be made by living cells. Proteins do not exist in air, like nitrogen or oxygen. They do not come directly from the sun, as with energy. In pollen, it is made by combining the nitrogen from nitrogen-containing materials from plants with carbon dioxide from the air and moisture. The plant uses the nitrogen from the air to combine with other substances to make protein.

What About Animal Foods?

They are good sources of protein but bee pollen offers you protein that is easily absorbed by the body without the animal fat.

Protein in Animal Foods

Meat (beef)	16.9 grams in 100 grams (about 3½ ounces)
Eggs	12.8 grams in 100 grams
Cheese	16.0 grams in 100 grams

Protein in Pollen

Mixed pollen: 19.7 grams in 100 grams of pollen

Amino Acids in Pollen

The following analytical table gives, a bit more precisely, comparisons of the protein contents of the amino acids. Serving size is 100 grams of pollen—or about 3½ ounces.

	ISOLEUCINE	LEUCINE	LYSINE	METHIONINE
Meat (beef)	0.93	1.28	1.45	0.42
Eggs	0.85	1.17	0.93	0.39
Cheese	1.74	2.63	2.34	0.80
Pollen	4.5	6.7	5.7	1.82

	PHENYLALANINE	THREONINE	TRYPTOPHAN	VALINE
Meat (beef)	0.66	0.81	0.20	0.91
Eggs	0.69	0.67	0.20	0.90
Cheese	1.43	1.38	0.34	2.05
Pollen	3.9	4.00	1.3	5.7

With one-half ounce of pollen a day, you should be able to give yourself the needed balance of amino acids for optimum health.

❖ The Power of Pollen for Healing

Dr. Varro E. Tyler, dean of the School of Pharmacy of Purdue University and author of *The New Honest Herbal*, has this to say about the life-giving power of pollen:

> *Although pollen extracts have been used for many years to detect and provide immunity against allergies, it is only during the past few years that pollen itself has become widely*

40

available in the form of tablets, capsules, extracts, and the like, which are recommended for a variety of ailments.

Pollen consists of microspores (male reproductive elements) of seed-bearing plants. Often the marketed product is designated bee pollen, implying that a mixture of pollens from various plants was collected by honeybees. Indeed, a mesh-like pollen trap has been developed which relieves bees of a portion of the pollen carried on their back legs as they reenter the hive.

Enthusiasts declare that pollen will either provide relief for or cure such conditions as premature aging, cerebral hemorrhage, bodily weakness, anemia, weight loss, enteritis, colitis and constipation. It is also said to have general tonic properties—promoting better health along with happiness and optimism. Studies conducted in Sweden and Japan seem to indicate the product may be of value in treating chronic prostatism. An Austrian report found pollen useful in alleviating the symptoms of radiation sickness in patients being treated for cancer of the cervix.[6]

❖ Bee Pollen + Honey = Better Health

James F. Balch, M.D., of Greenfield, Indiana, author of *Prescription for Nutritional Healing*, praises the benefits of bee pollen with honey for improved health.

Pollen is a fine powderlike material produced by the anthers of flowering plants, and gathered by the bees. Bee pollen

41

contains the B-complex vitamins, vitamin C, amino acids, polyunsaturated fatty acids, enzymes, carotene, calcium, copper, iron, magnesium, potassium, manganese, sodium and protein (10 to 35%). Bee pollen, bee propolis and honey have an antimicrobial effect. Honey is produced by the bee when plant nectar, which is a sweet substance secreted by flowers, is mixed with bee enzymes.

Honey varies in color and taste depending on the origin of flower and nectar. It contains 35% protein (one-half of all the amino acids) and is considered to be a complete food. It is a highly concentrated source of essential nutrients, containing large amounts of carbohydrates (sugars), the B-complex vitamins, vitamins C, D and E and some minerals. It is used to promote energy and healing.

Two tablespoons daily of honey is sufficient. It is twice as sweet as sugar and, therefore, not as much is needed. Only unfiltered, unheated, unprocessed honey should be purchased.

Diabetics and hypoglycemics should be careful when consuming honey and its by-products. The blood sugar reacts to these substances as it would to refined sugars. However, tupelo honey contains more levulose than any other honey and is absorbed at a slower rate so some hypoglycemics can use this type sparingly. If you are hypoglycemic, check with your health care provider. Do not feed honey to infants under one year of age, as they are more prone to develop botulism.

Dr. Balch adds that bee pollen is effective for combating fatigue, depression, cancer and colon disorders; it has an antimicrobial effect. He issues a warning: "Some people, approximately .05% may be allergic to pollen. Try small amounts at first and discontinue if a rash, wheezing, discomfort, or any other symptoms occur."[7]

❖ Healing With Pollen

Dr. Alfred Vogel, author of *The Nature Doctor*, has found pollen, as well as honey, to be a dynamic healer. He explains that pollen existed long before humans. The earth had to be prepared for survival of humans. For this reason, the plant world had to be made first, then came the animals and finally humans.

Pollen contains the male gametes of plants, which are essential to their propagation. Perhaps the wind carried these reproductive cells; otherwise the plants could not have been fertilized or pollinated before the arrival of insects.

When bees visit individual flowers with their untiring zeal in gathering nectar, they collect something else at the same time. Their little legs touch the pollen, which in turn sticks to them in tiny grains, making the bees look as if they were wearing tiny yellow pants. It is this pollen that is gathered. An analysis shows pollen to be rich in vitamins and to contain nearly all the minerals and trace elements vital to humans and beasts.

How can pollen be a healer? Dr. Vogel lists these discoveries:

Tiredness and Low Blood Pressure.

Experiments have shown that pollen has a strong action on the human sex glands and, through them, on all the endocrine glands. People who always feel tired and weary are able to get rid of this tiredness by taking a teaspoon of pollen in the morning with their breakfast.
Dr. Vogel says further,

> Pollen is excellent for low blood pressure, especially when taken together with seaweed, that is, kelp. If one drinks carrot juice in addition, the unpleasant symptoms of low blood pressure, for example, fainting and weakness, will usually be rectified after a short time. People who suffer from low blood pressure are often subject to sexual weakness, too, and therefore a deficiency in the sex glands. As a rule, taking pollen in combination with seaweed preparations can remedy this condition.

High Blood Pressure, Exophthalmic Goiter, Metabolic Disorders.

If the blood pressure is too high, it is not advisable to take pollen at the start, says Dr. Vogel.

A necessary precaution would be, first of all, to bring down the pressure by eating a natural diet of whole rice, soft white cheese (cottage cheese) and salads. Only when the blood pressure has been normalized can a person start taking pollen.

Those who have exophthalmic goiter, that is to say, a hyperfunction of the thyroid; should take pollen only after the functional disorder has been eliminated. On the other hand, metabolic disorders such as constipation and diarrhea can benefit from treatment with pollen.

Mental Strain.

Dr. Vogel finds that for those who do much mental work, bee pollen is an extremely simple and natural energy food.

With its help they are able to stand up to the intensity of their work for longer and feel less tired. In today's hustle and bustle of everyday life pollen is a welcome food supplement, providing the help needed when great demands are made on one's mental capacity.

Not all the active substances of pollen have yet been discovered, but those that have been isolated, as experience has shown, are cause enough to recommend this natural product to everyone who lives a modern life.

Bee pollen, being very rich in vitamins and containing all known minerals and trace elements, has become a popular energy booster. Since Nature provides us with this wonderful tonic food, we should prefer it to artificial or chemical products every time.[8]

❖ The President's Health Food

Former President Ronald W. Reagan reportedly would eat bee pollen regularly because it was an "energy restorative."

While he served as President, a supply of bee pollen was kept on hand not only in the White House but also aboard Air Force One, his private aircraft, and Executive One, the jet which transported Nancy Reagan on her missions throughout the country.

The bee pollen was in the form of a crunchy, 153-calorie snack bar. It is believed that this food "has rejuvenating properties which help cure fatigue, listlessness and ennui, as well as helping the President retain his natural hair color. No manufacturer of jelly beans, earlier publicized as Ronald Reagan's favorite candy, can equal that claim!"[9]

❖ Amazing Wonder Food

Leading medical journals throughout the world are praising the wonders of bee pollen—nature's most complete food. According to *How To Live the Millenium,* an encyclopedic work on the bee's health-giving products by Royden Brown, some of the amazing healing benefits include:

Russia, February 1990:

Patients with multiple sclerosis were given bee pollen to improve their powers of immunity.

Great Britain, January 1987:

Menopausal women were given a product containing bee pollen, royal jelly and vitamin C, for 30 days. Results:

82% of the women were symptom-free. The remaining 18% had symptoms reduced to a tolerable level. All told of feeling much better after only ten days of bee pollen.

Czechoslovakia, August 1987:

Patients with chronic renal insufficiency were given bee pollen and showed much improvement. Other reports told of the importance of bee pollen, iron and other nutrients that tend to improve the vigor and basic health of the patient.

Helps Ease Arteriosclerosis.

Kilmer McCully, M.D., as early as 1969, while at Harvard Medical School, noted that the original lesion (injury) in arteriosclerosis (heart disease) can be traced to a deficiency of vitamin B6 (pyridoxine) and an increase in homocysteine, a toxic substance. If allowed to accumulate, homocysteine, a breakdown product of the amino acid methionine, can be destructive. To counterattack, vitamin B6 is needed.

Dr. McCully noted that vitamin B6 facilitates the enzyme reaction which speedily transforms homocysteine to cystothionine, which is not toxic. "Since methionine is an essential amino acid—which means it must be on your plate every day," says Dr. McCully, "it would be in your best health interest to eat foods having a high B6 content and a low methionine content." The three foods having this heart-saving favorable B6-methionine ratio are:

> Bananas   ratio 40 to 1
> Carrots   ratio 15 to 1
> Onions   ratio 10 to 1

At that time, Dr. McCully was not aware that bee pollen has a B6-methionine ratio of 400 to 1. Later researchers found this to be true and it is possible that bee pollen may well help build immunity to heart disease, our number one health problem.

Why Is Bee Pollen So Special?

As explained, pollen is the male seed of flowers which fertilize a plant. Bees carry the pollen from one flower to another. The honeybee collects the pollen in a sac. Returning to the hive, the pollen grains which have not been deposited upon flowers are then placed in the honeycomb cell. Some fall on the bottom of the hive and this is the powerful wonder food gathered by beekeepers. In brief, it is a potent source of many valuable lifegiving and life extending nutrients.[10]

For example, bee pollen has the following rich treasures:

Rutin. This is a glucoside in bee pollen that increases the resistance of the capillary walls to infectious poisons. Pollen rutin will also help stabilize metabolism, which will improve respiration, emotional health and heart rhythm. It cuts down the time of bleeding so there is better healing and coagulation of the blood, and will reinforce the contraction of the heart and regulate its rhythm, which is most beneficial for heart health. Pollen rutin helps control hypertension by regulating the blood flow and soothing the nervous system.

DNA-RNA: Carriers of the genetic code; since the pollen is capable of reproduction, this is no surprise.

Hormones. Pollen contains sterols or plant hormones which can often take up the slack caused by diminishing endocrine activity. They also tend to activate the body glands and help them release a healthy supply of natural hormones for youthful longevity.

Antibiotic Factors. These substances found in bee pollen create a regulatory action on the intestinal region, produce improved blood health, calm and soothe the body through a healthy neuromuscular reaction. Toxic wastes and poisons are then neutralized through the antibiotic or disinfecting reaction of the pollen.

Vitamins. All known vitamins are present in a highly concentrated package to promote the various processes of the body, so that cell-tissue growth continues at a healthy rate, especially

Vitamin B12: not typically found in plant foods, it exists in a potent amount in bee pollen, making this an important food for those who avoid meat.

Vitamin E: very necessary for strengthening the heart, building the immune system.

Linoleic acid: an essential fatty acid not made by your body and needed for vascular health.

Glutamic acid: this nutrient crosses the blood/brain barrier, increases powers of intelligence and brain function. It may be useful in conditions of memory weakness.

Glucosides. These are natural sugars that combine with both the natural amount of fructose and glucose to create body energy and vitality.

Enzymes. Pollen contains many enzymes such as phosphatase, amylase and diastase which are needed to promote better metabolism and fermentation and transform food into youth-building elements. Enzymes will also use amino acids in the pollen and in the body for the rebuilding of body organs and revitalization of processes.

Analysis of Average Bee Pollen Content
reprinted from *Let's LIVE*, January 1981

Vitamins	Minerals	Enzymes, Co-enzymes
Provitamin A	Calcium	Amylase
Vitamin B1	Phosphorus	Diastase
Vitamin B2	Potassium	Saccharase
Niacin	Sulfur	Pectase
B6 group	Sodium	Phosphatase
Pantothenic acid	Chlorine	Catalase
Biotin	Magnesium	Disphorase
B12	Iron	Cozymase
Folic acid	Manganese	Cytochrome system
Choline	Copper	Lactic dehydrogenase
Inositol	Iodine	Succinic dehydrogenase
Vitamin C	Zinc	24 Oxidoreductases
Vitamin D	Silicon	21 Transferases
Vitamin E	Molybdenum	33 Hydrolases
Vitamin K	Boron	11 Lyases
Rutin	Titanium	5 Isomerases

Proteins, Amino Acids	Other	
Isoleucine	Nucleic acids	Hypoxalthine
Leucine	Flavonoids	Nuclein
Lysine	Phenolic acids	Amines

Proteins, Amino Acids	Other	
Methionine	Tarpenes	Lecithin
Phenylalanine	Nucleosides	Xanthophylls
Threonine	Auxins	Crocetin
Tryptophan	Fructose	Zeaxanthin
Valine	Glucose	Lycopene
Histidine	Brassins	Hexodecanal
Arginine	Gibberellins	Alpha-aminobutyric
Cysteine	Kinins	acid
Tyrosine	Vernine	Monoglycerides
Alanine	Xanthine	Diglycerides
Aspartic acid	Pentosans	Triglycerides
Glutamic acid		
Hydroxyproline		
Proline		
Serine	Plus: other ingredients still unclassified	

And do you wonder why bees have such powers of energy and are able to travel one million miles to the gallon of honey, for example? Because they eat some of the honey and pollen they have manufactured for energy to collect more nectar!

❖ Helps Boost the Immune System

Dr. Morton Walker in *Sexual Nutrition* says that in animals and human beings with an assortment of physical disorders, bee pollen has:

1. Revved up the energy of convalescents.
2. Regulated intestinal problems: both constipation and diarrhea.
3. Calmed, tranquilized and sedated patients with no side effects.
4. Increased the amount of blood hemoglobin (the oxygen-carrying factor), particularly in anemia.
5. Carried off impurities and toxins that accumulate in the capillaries, due to drugs, stress and to internal pollution from junk foods and environmental toxins.
6. Acted as a flushing agent or cleanser for artery-clogging toxic waste.

Eases Allergies.

Dr. Walker tells of William G. Peterson, M.D., a clinical allergist in Ada, Oklahoma, who recommended honeybee pollen to more than 22,000 patients throughout the country. Dr. Peterson says the bee pollen relieved allergy symptoms. When taken in small amounts, it helps build immunity to environmental pollution. He recommends that his patients prepare for the hay fever season a month in advance by taking a 2% concentrated solution of bee pollen in a glucose alcohol dilutent, starting with one drop daily and increasing by one drop daily until they reach 20 drops a day.

Once the allergy season starts, he advises them to increase the dosage by 5 drops daily until they reach 45 drops. Usually the range of treatment is between 20 and 70 drops daily. Some of Dr. Peterson's patients enjoy such dramatic relief, they are able to discontinue the treatment when they are healed.[11]

❖ Asthma—Breathe Free and Easy

Asthma, traditionally controlled (but not cured) by drugs, has responded to a honeybee pollen program. A researcher at Heidelberg University Children's Clinic in Germany, Ullrich Wahn, M.D., studied 70 children with hay fever and allergy-related asthma who drank a solution of bee pollen and honey daily during the annual hay fever period and three days weekly during the winter. Dr. Wahn reports, "Most of the children showed fewer symptoms after following this program, indicating that, in some mysterious way, the bee pollen made it into the bloodstream."[12]

❖ Athletes and Bee Pollen

In ancient days, bee pollen was the "ambrosia of the gods" and was a staple for Greek athletes girding their loins for the Olympics. This same ambrosia is now being fed to Olympian athletes who then go on to become winners, as in days of yore.

The Olympic athletes have discovered that they can improve their performances by taking bee pollen tablets. In particular, Finland trained over a thousand young men and women for the 1976 Olympics by giving them good food along with pollen supplements. These supplements were considered part of their training. The Finnish track coach, Antti Lananaki, told the press in the summer of 1976, "Most of our athletes take the bee pollen food supplement. Our

studies show that it significantly improves their performance. There have been no negative results since we began
supplying bee pollen to our athletes." Many Finnish runners
came away with awards, and it is believed that part of their
superior athletic power could be traced to the energizing
effect of bee pollen.

Another strong advocate of the use of bee pollen is Lasse
Viren, the Finnish star who won the 5000 and 10,000 meter
races in 1972 and again in 1976. He, too, attributed his
superior athletic vigor to the daily intake of bee pollen.

He took six to ten tablets a day during training, from
four to six tablets during competition.

Steve Riddick, Gold Medalist on the U.S. Relay Team at
Montreal in 1976, called bee pollen "fantastic" and credited
it for increasing his recovery power after a hard spring by
75 percent. "It gives me a lot more energy, too. I used to
take honey but this bee pollen is far better. I take three
pills a day."

As reported in the Long Island, New York newspaper
Newsday, entertainer Dick Gregory credited his stamina and
athletic ability to health foods such as wheat germ and vitamins but especially to bee pollen. "It gives you lightning
fast energy that will scare you to death." He said he was
able to run fifty miles a day and has this athletic ability
because of eating bee pollen along with other health foods.
He took chia seeds because they are one of nature's most
nutritious foods. They release energy already locked up in
the body. He also takes pumpkin seed oil, garlic capsules,
Korean ginseng and even sarsaparilla root, which he found
gave him strength.

Many coaches as well as athletes use bee pollen, which

they regard as energy in a capsule. As reported in *Let's Live* (July 1976), here are some of the athletic-boosting benefits of this natural food:

After his track team had been given bee pollen for four months, trainer Jack Gimmler at St. John's University, Queens, New York, was so convinced of the performance of his athletes that he was able to persuade the university to underwrite a year's supply for sixty athletes—including track, basketball and swimming.

At Seton Hall University in New Jersey, athletes were put on a three-month program of taking bee pollen. Coach Jim Moon was able to build up their vigor so that the athletes set a U.S. indoor track record for the mile relay in Detroit. Later, the same bee-pollen-energized athletes took top honors at the Metropolitan Intercollegiate Indoor Track and Field Championships at Princeton.

Trainer Doug Boyd at Fairleigh Dickinson University in Rutherford, New Jersey, gives bee pollen to his athletes, who have many winning scores to their credit.

Coach Tommy Smith at Oberlin in Ohio also gives bee pollen to his budding athletes. More research is being conducted to determine whether this energizing food should be given to athletes throughout the country, and the world.

"Athletes as diverse as Olympic distance runners and professional basketball players are popping tablets of pollen at the rate of five or 10 a day," says *The New York Times* (February 6, 1977). "John Williamson, the high-scoring guard traded by the Nets to Indiana this week, says his 10 tablets a day give him this burst of energy on the court he did not even know he had."

Dr. Roger Morse, professor of apiculture at Cornell University, said, "People have been eating bee pollen for hundreds of years. It's a good, rich source of protein."

Dr. Charles W. Turner, head trainer for Long Island University, traveled throughout the world and came upon bee pollen in 1973 while in Europe. He feels bee pollen does provide energy and vigor for athletes. He also uses bee pollen as a poultice to reduce swelling of the limbs that frequently occurs among athletes. He dissolves pollen pellets in warm tap water until they form an infusion. He dips a towel in the mixture and applies it to the injured region. Dr. Turner says, "I've seen swelling go down a half inch in twenty minutes because of this pollen poultice. I've seen results on all but two of the 189 knees, ankles and the like that were given this pollen poultice."

A Long Island University gymnast, Brigitte Bouchereau, underwent cartilage surgery on her knees. She went on a bee pollen program, both internal and external (in the form of a poultice), and says, "I've improved a lot. My knees are 100 percent better."

Dr. Turner says, "I know I'll have trouble with the medical people on this. There are too many big shots among doctors. They don't have time to listen to small cases. If the treatment worked only 50 percent of the time, they'd accept it.

"We are pollen people. We believe it. . . . We want to get a certain amount of medical men involved in the experiments, but we don't feel we're quite ready yet."

At age 37, George Stillman was able to run 52½ miles from the New York side of the George Washington Bridge to Middletown Township, New Jersey, in seven hours and 40 minutes. This former Asbury Park (New Jersey) High

School and Universty of Maryland athlete was able to run with good mental and physical stamina, during severe weather, *subsisting exclusively on just one food item—bee pollen.* Two aides followed him via automobile and kept him energized with bee pollen pellets.

As reported in the *Asbury Park Press* (January 23, 1977), George Stillman originally planned this special run on December 26, 1976, as his parting salute to the Bicentennial year and American awareness of physical fitness.

But there was a very heavy snow and ice storm, so he had to postpone this 52½-mile run until January 16, 1977. Even so, when this bee-pollen-nourished athlete went across the George Washington Bridge, he was greeted by light snow flurries in twenty-four-degree weather . . . hardly a climate conducive to running, especially for a man of thirty-seven, considered to be out of his prime by current youthful standards. But George Stillman would not be delayed. He started to run, even though there were frozen roadways and slippery conditions. He started to slow in a semijog, then went to an occasional speed walk.

"The temperature was still dropping as I got past the Amboys. My muscles started to pull in the thighs and the back. And I have a lower left lumbar condition to start off with." Soon, he said, he had "cold and stiffness through my arms, legs and shoulders. The whole left side of me seemed strained." But he persisted. Stillman credits his energy and vitality in being able to complete the 52½-mile run in bad weather to bee pollen.

Les Wallach, a coach at Rutgers University, gave bee pollen to his track athletes over a period of time. The runners went on to win the New Jersey cross-country championship for the first time. In November 1976, the cross-country team won the Metropolitan Intercollegiate Cross-Country Championship in New York. After forty-eight years of running *without winning a single title*, the athletes started to gather up championships. Coach Wallach, as reported in the *New Brunswick* (N.J.) *Home News* (November 8, 1976), attributed their sudden winning streak to good training as well as to bee pollen. Said Coach Wallach:

> *No one makes any claims that bee pollen is beneficial, but I think that it is. I take it myself. I feel great. I've had no head colds, a lot more vitality and I find I am sleeping more restfully.*
>
> *Others have told me of claims for bee pollen. I heard about it after the 1972 Olympics, recommended it for my track team to add nutrients because I felt they might not be eating the proper foods while carrying a heavy workload as students and athletes.*

Bee pollen is especially rich in a potent member of the B-complex vitamin group, namely, pantothenic acid, which has a key role in metabolism, for antibody formation and also for the stimulus of the nervous system. This vitamin helps the body build resistance to stress and has a healthy and natural influence on the production of the adrenal-cortical hormones. When the glandular system is adequately nourished with sufficient pantothenic acid as found in bee pollen, it does create a powerhouse of vitality and energy. This may be one of the many reasons why it is able to stimulate athletes of different ages to transform them from average runners to champions.

Athletic Coach Cheers Bee Pollen

Tom McNab, who was the official athletics coach to the British athletic teams, was responsible for the training of members of the national team and for ensuring that they consumed a diet suitable for their athletic activities.

Coach McNab said, "I frequently test food supplements alleged by their manufacturers to assist athletes in reaching their optimum physical condition. To test the efficacy of one of these supplements, I ask a number of athletes training under either my supervision or that of other coaches to take the supplement in accordance with the manufacturer's recommendations. I then carefully monitor the athletic performance of the athletes to see whether any improvement in their ability results from taking the product tested. . . .

> I was asked to test the efficacy of a bee pollen product. I was initially skeptical of the results likely to be obtained by use of this product. However, I asked five athletes training under me to take bee pollen in accordance with the manufacturer's directions; that is, one to three pills a day. Within a period of 12 months, the athletic performance of all of the five athletes taking bee pollen had substantially improved.

Here are the results:

The best performance of a female hurdler, age twenty-eight, prior to taking bee pollen was 13.3 seconds. After taking the pollen, training levels rose immediately. She improved to 12.9 seconds and won a Commonwealth Games Gold Medal.

When a male decathlete, age eighteen, started taking bee pollen, his body weight went up eight pounds, and within four weeks, there was a big rise in his weight-training capacity. Personal performances improved in training.

Before taking bee pollen, the best performance of a twenty-five-year-old female hurdler was 14.1 seconds. Soon she improved to 13.6 seconds and achieved a good position on the British team. There was a noticeable improvement in her work rate.

Before taking bee pollen, the best performance of a male javelin thrower, age twenty-three, was 210 feet. After taking bee pollen, he improved to 235 feet 6 inches. Again, a big improvement in work rate, weight and muscle mass was noted.

Before taking bee pollen, the best performance of a twenty-four-year-old male hurdler was 51.8 seconds. After taking bee pollen, he improved to 50.7 seconds. He gained a well-deserved place in the Commonwealth Games Team. He considers bee pollen to be an essential part of his training diet.

Coach Tom McNab concludes:

> The main value of bee pollen is not just in its direct effect upon performance, but rather in its apparent effect upon training levels. This rise in training levels enables more work to be done, more skill to be acquired and more muscle to be developed.
>
> The effect of bee pollen is particularly notable in underweight athletes. Both the javelin thrower and the decathlete noted an immediate (that is, within two weeks) rise in bodyweight and lean muscle mass.
>
> It is usually presumptuous to ascribe improvement to any single factor. However, I believe that bee pollen has had a significant effect on the cases described, especially on the last-

named male hurdler, whose work rate improvement was dramatic.

A beneficial side effect which I attribute to bee pollen has been the diminution of the number of colds which the athletes have experienced. Freedom from such complaints is a major factor in any training program.

I conclude that bee pollen is the most effective revitalizing food supplement available to athletes today of all the food supplements which I have tested.

Mr. McNab said that, among the track and field athletes he trained for the Olympics, "At least 90 percent of our athletes are taking bee pollen tablets daily. Most claim that it improves their performance, and gives them greater stamina and more energy."

To boost your own stamina and energy, to help revitalize your body and mind so that you can enjoy the best that life has to offer you, take bee pollen daily. You may not become a Gold Medal champion or Olympic winner, but you will feel like one.

❖ Easy Ways to Use Pollen.

◆ Sprinkle bee pollen grains on your morning whole grain cereal.

◆ Mix the grains with freshly prepared fruit juices.

◆ Spread on a slice of whole grain bread.

◆ Blend with applesauce, salad dressing, cottage cheese.

Bee pollen is nature's most complete food. It alone can

sustain life. It is the bread of the bees and is the beehive's main food. Gathered from the stamen of flowers, it contains up to 25% complete vegetable protein plus an assortment of virtually all vitamins and minerals together with enzymes and co-enzymes, carbohydrates and essential fatty acids. It is low in fats and calories. Nature takes care of this "food combining." That is, the nutrients in bee pollen are found together in a natural balance. Bee pollen is readily absorbed and rapidly assimilated by the body.

❖ How Perfect Is Pollen?

G. J. Binder, medical researcher-author of *About Pollen*, considers this food to be just about perfect.

> *Pollen proves to be the most health-giving strength and energy restorer of all foods from the beehive. What proves most gratifying about pollen is that it is not only non-addictive but causes not the slightest ill or side effects to persons taking it, even over long periods.*

Complete Source of Sustenance.

Furthermore, Binder tells us that pollen has shown itself to be a complete nourishment in every sense of the word. It would prove hard, almost impossible in fact, to find a food from animal or vegetable sources containing such vital elements. Not only does it build up strength and energy in tired bodies, but it acts as a tonic.

For people who have temporarily lost the zest for living, a course of pollen may well be the answer to their problems. French doctors have noted that in less than a week in practically every case, pollen restores normal healthy appetites to people who previously have seldom enjoyed meals. This is perhaps why in most cases it increases the bodyweight of under-developed persons.

Strangely enough, pollen was also found to help weight reduction for people who were fat, proving that pollen is an ideal body regulator in every possible way. The new food was shown to stimulate many functions of the body, including the gastric system. Containing a natural antibiotic, it also controls dangerous bacteria in the intestines. The benefits experienced by persons given pollen by French doctors not only consisted of restored bodily health, but also a more optimistic outlook on life, which is so often closely related to physical harmony. It is pollen that gives people more vigor, vitality and increased resistance to infection.[13]

❖ Common and Uncommon Healing Remedies

Throughout human history honey and pollen have been used for healing. Here are some folk remedies from past and present times:

Detoxification.

Take several tablespoons of honey and pollen daily for body detoxification and inner cleansing. These bee-made foods are high in potassium (among other nutrients) which creates a hygroscopic reaction (the ability to draw off excess moisture). Because germs and free radical molecules thrive in moisture, this detoxification will help cleanse them from your system; deprived of moisture-nourishment, they die and can be eliminated easily.

Wounds, Burns, Boils.

Egyptians applied honey to raw wounds to boost healing. Orientals applied an ointment of honey and pollen to skin blemishes for clearing. Physicians of the ancient world would combine honey with pollen and use as a dressing on top of ulcerated wounds, burns, boils and skin problems.

Folk Healing with Honey and Pollen.

South American Indians would apply honey and pollen as a dressing to various skin disorders. Farm people of the Slavic region of Europe would combine honey, pollen and flour to use as a natural ointment upon wounds and burns. Norse explorers used a sprinkling of pollen on burns and wounds to facilitate healing. In modern times, Scandinavian people combine honey, pollen and a bit of fish liver oil to use as an ointment on blemishes.

Respiratory Ailments.

In many regions of Europe, natives use a combination of honey and pollen to help heal respiratory disorders. It is sipped slowly from a teaspoon to soothe the itching throat. It is also said to heal bronchial disorders as well as allergies such as asthma; a honey-pollen poultice is often applied around the throat. A few drops of slightly warmed honey-pollen in the ear eases pain and ringing or inflammation.

Honey + Pollen + Warm Milk = Healthy Throat.

Many public speakers and entertainers will soothe an overworked throat with this combination. Sip slowly and you'll feel yourself speaking in golden tones.

Respiratory Relief.

Folklorists suggest you dissolve 1 tablespoon of honey, 1 teaspoon bee pollen and some lemon juice in a cup of freshly boiled water. Stir vigorously until dissolved. Sip slowly when tepid. This mixture reportedly soothes respiratory distress, sore throat and other symptoms of lung discomfort.

Natural Sleeping Tonic.

Early New England settlers prepared this mixture: combine 4 tablespoons honey, 2 teaspoons pollen, 3 teaspoons apple cider vinegar in a cup of freshly boiled water. Sip slowly when tepid. Taken especially at bedtime, it is said to be a delightful all-natural sleeping tonic.

Oriental Youth Elixir.

Combine 2 tablespoons honey, 2 teaspoons pollen, ½ teaspoon chopped ginseng herb and ¼ teaspoon dried orange peel. Take with a spoon. Oriental healers believe it creates a feeling of total rejuvenation and vitality.

Natural Regularity.

Troubled by constipation? Look to the beehive for natural help. When you take honey with pollen, either in liquids or as a topping on thick black bread, your metabolism becomes stabilized, relieving constipation or diarrhea and you enjoy healthy regularity.

Improves Digestion.

Bee pollen is a natural way to help correct problems of the digestive system and restore a feeling of youthfulness to this entire region. Because pollen consists of an inverted sugar, it does not ferment or "sour" in the digestive tract. It is speedily absorbed, helps keep out bacterial invasion and has a demulcent (soothing) effect on irritated or inflamed intestines. By its natural lubricating power and natural fatty acid content, bee pollen stimulates sluggish peristalsis, resulting in regularity without the need for laxatives and in elimination of bulk with less strain.

Bee pollen is a rapidly acting source of muscular energy and promotes a restorative reaction to the digestive system. The pollen will activate digestive muscles so that they are able to consume four times as much energy-creating glycogen as when at rest, thus invigorating the digestive system. When bee pollen is taken by itself, without food, it appears to work unhindered in correcting errors of metabolism which may be involved in unhealthy weight gain. Here is how this works to control weight:

Sugars and fats are both energy-providing and carbon-containing foods; when they combine with oxygen, they burn up to produce energy. Sugars are higher in carbon elements; they are flammable and produce this energy very quickly. Fats are lower in carbon and oxygen elements than sugars. Therefore, fats are metabolized slower because their function is to supply reserve energy. Fats need more oxygen to be set afire to be put into reserve for future use.

When bee pollen inverted sugars are taken into your digestive system, there is a speedy combustion. The fats will burn with the help of oxygen produced by their "fire." This causes a speedy increase in the rate of sugar metabolism and there is an increased rate of calorie burning and consequent weight loss. It is bee pollen which causes this internal reaction. It is the natural way to improve metabolism and help control and take off weight

Those who have put much store in the effects of lactic acid would do well to consider bee pollen as a complementary source of digestive healing. Says Dr. Paavo O. Airola in *Health Secrets From Europe:*

> *It has been suggested that Bulgarians, Rumanians, Russians and other East European peoples known for their enviable record of longevity have to thank lactic acid for their excellent health and youthful vitality. Their diets are high*

in soured foods (rich in lactic acid) such as sour milk, yogurt,
black sourdough bread, sauerkraut and the like. Lactic acid
has a beneficial anti-putrefactive effect on the intestines and
keeps the digestive tract in good health.

Probably the most beneficial effect of pollen is that, taken
internally, it quickly produces the same anti-putrefactive ef-
fect as lactic acid foods, and thus contributes to a healthy
digestive system and good assimilation of nutrients—absolute
prerequisites for good health and long life.

A dramatic case of the digestive-satisfying powers of bee
pollen is offered by U.S. Air Force Lieutenant Colonel Thomas
J. Tretheway. As reported in *The Golden Pollen* (Yakima, Wash.:
Yakima Binding and Printing Company, 1960), during World
War II, this paratrooper escaped from a Japanese prison camp
in Burma. Natives helped Tretheway escape. They were inter-
ested in traveling speedily so did not weigh themselves down
with food. Instead, whenever they came to a stream, they
would skim floating pollen off the water, offer a good portion
to Tretheway and eat much of it themselves. Tretheway says
they went through the rigors of jungle traveling and ate absolutely nothing but pollen. This satisfied them. All were healthy,
energetic and youthful. He even regained weight he lost in
prison camp on a diet solely of pollen.

Colonel Tretheway reported that he and the natives either ate the pollen by itself or else they would mix it with
honey and eat it in the form of a cake. He says, "All of
them were tall, slender, had perfect teeth. Youngsters and
adults appeared to be in perfect health on a staple diet of
pollen. I, too, felt healthy from this exclusive and sole fare."

Tretheway said that when he developed gangrene-like

feet, the natives would coat his wounds with a poultice of pollen and honey, which promoted speedy healing. When Tretheway eventually made it to safety in Calcutta, he was told by a British physician that he had to thank pollen and honey because they saved his feet . . . and his life!

Later, Tretheway told his superiors that pollen was such a complete or all-purpose or "perfect" food that it was an excellent survival food—someone could live on it and remain in good digestive health and survive even in the total absence of all other food.

Improves Muscular Vigor.

The billions of cells and tissues in your muscles require sugar for energy. When muscles are active, they use up nearly four times as much glycogen as when at rest. It is a biological-scientific discovery that predigested sugars in bee pollen convert rapidly in the bloodstream to glycogen. Almost immediately after taking it, there is a speedy natural carbohydrate assimilation. Nourishment is dispatched to your hungry muscle cells and tissues, rewarding you with energy and vigor.

Kidney-Bladder Revitalization.

Take honey with pollen on one spoon or mix it with a fruit or vegetable juice for natural diuretic action. For problems of pyelitis (inflammation of the kidneys), honey helps prompt the release of urine, thereby detoxifying both the kidneys and the bladder to create a beneficial antiseptic reaction.

Sore Throat.

Many professional speakers and singers use honey and pollen to clear away obstructions in the throat. A popular throat-pleaser is prepared by mixing 3 parts honey with 1 part pollen and 1 part compound tincture of benzoin (available at herbal pharmacies.) Take by the teaspoon. It feels smooth as it goes down the throat, sweeping away phlegm.

Soothing Gargle.

Folklorists suggest adding 1 tablespoon pollen, 3½ ounces honey and 1 ounce rose hips powder to 1 quart water. Stir until thoroughly blended. Then gargle with this mixture at various times of the day. Soothes itchy, scratchy throats.

From the earliest days, man has been searching for a substance that will help perpetuate the look and feel of youth. His search has almost always led him to the beehive and products made by these winged creatures who appear to predate man. Bees have a built-in survival power that has made them among nature's oldest surviving creatures. The secret for their stamina may well be in the hive—in the form of honey and even more in the form of pollen.

❖ Your Pollen Program

Bee pollen comes from many different floral sources. Just as with honey, bee pollen comes in all colors and tastes. Some may be a little sweet. Other pollen may have a tangy taste. But all bee pollen is a source of healthful energy and healing powers. Therefore, experiment with different varieties until you find the one you like. Or else use variations throughout the week so your body system can be rewarded with different potencies, different flavors. Health stores and pharmacies have all varieties of bee pollen available for your personal satisfaction.

For better assimilation, take pollen before eating. Take whatever amount is prescribed on the box or bottle, since each form and variety differs from every other. But always be consistent in your schedule—stick to it. Pollen appears to be better absorbed and more speedily assimilated when it is taken before a meal, so make this your rule of thumb.

Follow label directions on how much to use. Depending on your personal requirements, you may want more or less potent doses than indicated. If you feel you need more protective measures or if you want to build stronger immunity to the threat of illness, then increase the amount of pollen. When your health has been built up, take maintenance dosage daily. Again, this is determined only by your individual needs and feelings. And again, read labels.

Here are some suggestions on how to take the bee pollen:

- Chew the pellets slowly, as they are, and swallow with a drink.
- Take the prescribed number of tablets or capsules with a fresh fruit or vegetable juice, hot beverage or a glass of water. Drink slowly.
- Sprinkle one teaspoonful of grains on any fruit or vegetable salad.

+ Sprinkle the pollen grains into yogurt or cereal.
+ Mix with honey, health jam or marmalade and spread atop whole-grain bread.
+ Sprinkle pollen grains in fruit cocktails or on fruit salads or in a gelatin dessert.
+ Add pollen grains to any beverage made with a juice extractor or blender.
+ *Most important:* establish your pollen-taking program and stick to it daily.
+ You should not cook pollen as this will destroy many of the valuable substances contained within. You can, however, add the pellets to a food or liquid which is slightly warm.

❖ Look Younger With Bee Pollen

Your skin can look younger, be free of wrinkles, smoother and healthier with the use of bee pollen. This is the discovery made by Lars-Erik Essen, M.D., of Hälsingborg, Sweden who is considered a pioneer in the use of this rejuvenating food.

As a dermatologist, Dr. Essen treated many of his patients for blemishes. He developed a pollen lotion that could help inhibit skin disorders and also smooth down and erase wrinkles and furrows.

Dr. Essen explains,

> *Pollen seems to prevent premature aging of the skin and stimulates growth of new skin tissue, offering effective*

protection against dehydration. The complexion becomes younger looking, less vulnerable to wrinkles, smoother and healthier with the use of bee pollen. It promotes a cleansing effect on acne. French research concurs that pollen contains elements which can reverse the aging of the skin and correct darkening, wrinkles and blemishes.

How Pollen Clears Up Skin.

Furthermore, Dr. Essen notes that not only does pollen help clear up acne conditions in the young, but it is also of special benefit in skin rejuvenation for older people.

Through transcutaneous nutrition, bee pollen has a profound biological effect. It seems to prevent premature aging of the cells and stimulates the growth of new skin tissue. It offers effective protection against dehydration and injects new life into dry cells. It smooths away wrinkles and stimulates the life-giving blood supply to all skin cells.[14]

Bee pollen is an important skin rejuvenator because it contains a rich concentration of the nucleic acids, DNA and RNA, the genetic code. These substances penetrate the surface of the skin when a lotion containing bee pollen is applied; they nourish the cells and tissues beneath. They act as a moisturizer for dry skin subject to wrinkling and premature aging; they also smooth furrows and creases.

Improve the look and feel of your skin and hair with bee pollen in a variety of all-natural beauty preparations you can make at home at a cost of only pennies. Here is an assortment of folk remedies that use bee pollen as an ingredient together with other natural foods that help revitalize and rejuvenate your body so you will glow with youthful alertness.

At your local health store or pharmacy, obtain bee pollen in pellet form. Break open the pellet and let the tiny grains spill out onto a spoon for specific measurements. Or purchase free-flowing pollen grains from your health store or pharmacy. Use the grains as soon after purchase as possible when they are fresh and potent.

✦ FACIAL CLEANSER ✦

Beat the yolk of an egg until it is light and frothy. Add ½ cup milk, ½ mashed ripe avocado and 1 teaspoon bee pollen grains. A blender is handy here, but if not available, beat the mixture with a fork until you have a thin cream or lotionlike consistency. Apply with cotton squares as you would any other cleanser.

You may also use this deeper cleanser after ordinary soap and water. If your skin is normal, it is a very good way of keeping your complexion free of pollutants and toxic grime which can cause premature aging. Since this formula is perishable, it is best to make it every other day and store in the refrigerator between uses.

✦ SPICE ASTRINGENT ✦

In a measuring cup, combine 2 tablespoons lemon juice, 1 tablespoon glycerin and 1 tablespoon 70% alcohol. Add 1 tablespoon bee pollen grains, then enough distilled witch hazel to fill the

*cup to the 8-ounce level. Stir vigorously with a spoon. Refriger-
ate only until tingly cool. Then apply with your fingertips.
Let the astringent soak into your pores throughout the day.*

◆ SKIN PEP TONIC ◆

*Combine 2 tablespoons buttermilk, 1 teaspoon bee pollen
grains and four tablespoons tomato juice in a blender or else
hand-stir vigorously. Apply to your skin with cotton pads. Let
remain up to 30 minutes, then splash off with cool water.*

◆ FACE SCRUB ◆

*Peel and mash half of a ripe avocado. Mix it with ½ cup
yellow or white fine-grind cornmeal. Add 1 tablespoon bee
pollen grains. Now, thoroughly wash your face in warm
and then cold water. Next, rub this mixture into the trouble
spots on your face. Continue rubbing (gently) for 10 minutes. Then remove with a damp washcloth and splash your
face with cold water. The grains, combined with the other
ingredients, help slough off dead skin tissues, smooth out
wrinkles and erase crease lines.*

◆ HERB RINSE ◆

*To a cup of freshly boiled water, add ¼ cup fresh parsley,
one teaspoon dried peppermint leaves, 1 teaspoon bee pollen grains. Let steep at least 30 minutes. Now strain*

through a cheesecloth. Pour into a clean glass bottle. Use as an after-rinse, following your washing.

◆ NECK–JAWLINE REJUVENATOR ◆

Puree ½ avocado. Stir into it 1 tablespoon fresh wheat germ oil and 1 tablespoon bee pollen grains. You should now have a smooth cream. Rub this cream into your neck and jawline areas with firm strokes, going up and down, then down and up. When most of the cream has been absorbed, remove the excess and leave on the film for at least an hour or, better yet, overnight. Use daily or nightly.

◆ PORE TIGHTENER ◆

In a clean bottle, combine 4 tablespoons rose water, ½ teaspoon spirits of camphor, one teaspoon bee pollen grains and two teaspoons alcohol (70% strength). Shake thoroughly until combined and keep in cool place. To use, apply with cotton pads over the entire skin area, rubbing into those sections which have large pores. Let soak in overnight. Next morning, splash off with cool water.

◆ DRY SKIN MASK ◆

Beat an egg yolk until it is light and frothy. Then add the mashed pulp of ½ avocado and 2 tablespoons bee pollen grains, blending them together thoroughly. Wash your face and throat before applying this mask. Now spread the mixture over your face and neck evenly; relax on a slant board or a bed for about 20 minutes. Splash off with clear, tepid water and dry with a facecloth; follow with a rinse of cold water.

◆ OILY SKIN MASK ◆

Put the white of an egg, 1 teaspoon lemon juice, 2 teaspoons bee pollen grains and the mashed pulp of ½ avocado into a blender. In seconds, you should have a lovely seagreen mixture. Or else beat vigorously by hand with a spoon. Wash your face and neck very thoroughly, then apply the mask evenly. Relax for 20 minutes; remove with tepid water and a facecloth. Finish with a cold astringent.

◆ HEALTHIER HAIR ◆

Add a few drops of freshly squeezed lemon juice and ½ teaspoon of bee pollen grains to your favorite shampoo. Then use as usual. Your hair will have a new, shiny and vibrant appearance.

◆ SOFTER FEET ◆

Soak your feet in a mixture of comfortably warm water, 1 teaspoon bee pollen grains and the juice of 1 lemon.

Enjoy the soak until the water starts to cool. Then rinse off in warm and cool water and dry carefully.

◆ POLLEN SCRUB ◆

About once a week, your face should be given a good scrubbing to clear up the dull, muddy look that comes from pollution and toxic assault, as well as excess oils that accumulate throughout the day. Here's how to prepare your pollen scrub: mix together the juice of 1 lemon and the white of 1 egg. Add 1 teaspoon bee pollen grains. Now add dry oatmeal gradually until you have a soft paste. Mix with a slight chopping motion, then allow to set a few minutes until the moisture is absorbed. Apply to your face, avoiding areas around the eyes. Rub in gently with a very tender scrubbing motion. Let dry about 10 minutes, then rinse off with clear, warm water.

◆ ICE RUB ◆

To give your face a refreshing pick-me-up on a hot day, fill an ice cube tray with equal parts strained lemon juice and water and 3 tablespoons bee pollen grains. Freeze. Whenever you want to refresh your face, remove one of the cubes and lightly rub over your face and neck. Rinse with cold water and pat dry. Your face will feel as refreshed as if you'd splashed it in a sparkling mountain stream.

◆ POLLEN YOUTH BATH ◆

Fill a tub with comfortably warm water. Add ½ cup bee pollen grains and one sliced lemon. The lemon oils will release their fragrance and combine with the nectar-scented aroma of the grains to make you feel as if you are in a luxurious enchanted forest, bathing in an ambrosia-filled stream. Indulge yourself for 30 to 45 minutes in this pollen youth bath. Emerge with the radiant glow of youthful health and vitality.

◆ SALT POLLEN RUBDOWN ◆

This is a wonderful way to smooth your body skin. This pre-bath or pre-shower program is very stimulating. It is a great help in removing and healing blemishes on your shoulders and back. It may be too strong for your delicate facial tissues, so test on an inconspicuous portion of your face as large as a coin. If no irritation is felt, use gently on the rest of your skin.

Mash ½ peeled avocado with ½ cup ordinary table salt and 2 tablespoons bee pollen grains. When thoroughly combined, rub the entire mixture all over your body, with particular emphasis on trouble spots. Use gentle friction. (Do it in your tub or shower stall.) Dead skin will slough off in a miraculous way, especially from your feet, knees and elbows. When you think you've had enough, shower off and then bathe as usual.

◆ POLLEN SOAP SUBSTITUTE ◆

Mix together 1 egg yolk, 1 tablespoon glycerin, 1 teaspoon bee pollen grains. Gently pat onto your face. Let dry. Then splash off with warm water. Keep a supply in a closed jar in your refrigerator. (Always shake well before using.) This is a skin-nourishing substitute for those who do not want abrasive soap on their skin.

◆ NIGHT BODY OIL ◆

Combine 1 tablespoon each: sesame oil, light olive oil, safflower oil, corn oil and bee pollen grains. Add 3 drops oil of bitter almonds (from herbal pharmacist) and shake together very thoroughly in a glass bottle. After your evening shower or bath (when your body pores are still open from the warm steam vapors), apply this overnight body oil onto your skin in a very light film. Rub gently deep into your skin. Then put on your nightclothes and enjoy a good night's sleep. Next morning, shower or bathe with tepid water and finish with a cool splash. Your skin should have a silky soft feeling. Repeat frequently to be rewarded with a healthy skin that glows with youthful radiance.

◆ DANDRUFF-AWAY LOTION ◆

In a glass bottle, shake together 1 cup white vinegar, 1 cup water, 3 tablespoons bee pollen grains. Dab this solution, using cotton pads, onto your scalp before shampooing. Rub

80

it in well. When your entire scalp and hair have been covered, wash your hair with your favorite shampoo. (A baby shampoo or one that is free of chemicals is preferred.) Ingredients in this lotion help loosen scalp debris and cleanse your skin, so your hair looks and feels squeaky clean.

◆ DRY HAIR POLLEN TREATMENT ◆

In ½ cup mayonnaise (or mayonnaise-type salad dressing) stir 1 teaspoon bee pollen grains. Gently massage this mixture into your scalp and hair. Let it soak up to 30 minutes to allow it to penetrate; rinse under tepid water, then shampoo. This treatment helps moisturize scalp cells and improve the health of dry hair. Repeat three times a week.

◆ SCALP NOURISHING TONIC ◆

Simmer 1 cup water. Into this add 1 tablespoon flaxseed oil and 1 teaspoon bee pollen grains. Puncture 1 vitamin A and 1 vitamin E capsule and squeeze the contents into the simmering water. Stir until ingredients are dissolved. Let the mixture cool until it is comfortable to the touch but still warm. Apply to scalp and hair with fingertips. Cover your head with a plastic shower cap to seal in body warmth and keep scalp pores open so this tonic can "feed" your hair follicles. After 30 minutes, remove cap and rinse your hair under tepid water. Shampoo as customary. Repeat three times per week. Nutrients in this *scalp-nourishing tonic feed your hair follicles and promote healthier hair.*

❖ Is Bee Pollen a Miracle Food?

This question was asked of the late Dr. Paavo Airola, internationally recognized nutritionist, naturopathic physician and past President of the International Academy of Biological Medicine.

Dr. Airola had this answer:

The miraculous powers of pollen were recognized by man since early history. Ancient texts from Egypt, Persia and China refer to it. Greek philosophers claimed that pollen held the secret of eternal youth. It was revered as Nature's own propagator of life.

Pollen is the male germ cells of the flowering plants. Bees collect pollen to feed the young working bees that produce royal jelly, the exclusive food of the Queen bee. The analysis of pollen has shown that it is indeed a food for the gods—it is the richest and most complete food in nature!

It contains 20% complete protein, all the water-soluble vitamins, a rich supply of minerals and trace elements, and enzymes and coenzymes. The other vital substances are so-called deoxyribosides and stearines, plus traces of steroid hormone substances.

There is much research from various countries showing

that pollen possesses remarkable medicinal properties. Swedish and French researchers have used it successfully in treatment of chronic prostate inflammation, hemorrhoids, digestive disorders, constipation, asthma, allergies, hay fever, and colonic infections.

It has been demonstrated that pollen increases the body's own immunity and also stimulates and rejuvenates its glandular activity. It has been used as a general tonic in convalescence and in the treatment of symptoms of aging. It is considered to be totally harmless.[15]

❖ How to Heal Your Allergies With Bee Pollen

Many allergies, such as asthma or hay fever, are caused by pollen introduced into the respiratory system. But scientists have found that bee pollen can help build immunity and that there is a difference between inhaled pollen and the bee pollen product.

Allergies are caused generally by breathing in the anemophilous pollens which are carried by the wind. To help build a form of natural immunity, your body requires a supply of entomophilous pollens (gathered by the bees from a variety of different blossoms) that will act as a barrier or shield against the windborne and inhaled pollens that are responsible for your allergic reaction. The bee-collected pollens are often very sticky and heavy and cannot be carried by the wind. These pollens are healing because when the bees form them into pellets, they add a little nectar and saliva. This neutralizes and destroys any allergic principle (if one existed) and makes bee pollen a respiratory-strengthening food that can help heal and even prevent allergies. By taking one teaspoon of bee pollen daily, resistance to wind-carried pollen is slowly built up and the sensitivity to allergy is reduced. Gradually, your body builds up a shield to insulate you from the irritating effects of wind-carried pollen.

The ability of bee pollen to immunize the body against allergies was reported in the *Florida Farmers Bulletin* (October 15, 1969) under the title, "Doctors Recommend Raw Honey Treatment for Allergies":

An Oklahoma allergist told a meeting of 150 beekeepers that raw honey is an effective treatment for 90 percent of all allergies. Dr. William G. Peterson, an allergist from Ada, Oklahoma, said he now has 22,000 patients across the nation who are using raw honey—along with more customary medication—to relieve allergic symptoms.

It must be raw honey, because raw honey contains all the pollen, dust, and molds that cause 90 percent of all allergies. What happens is that the patient builds up an immunity to the pollen, dust or mold that is causing his trouble in the first place, Dr. Peterson told the meeting of the Oklahoma Beekeepers Association.

"The raw honey must not be strained, not even through a cloth. I know the customer wants good, clear, strained, filtered honey and that's fine, but for health reasons, raw honey is what we need.

"*Along with myself, there are 20 doctors at my clinic in Ada who normally prescribe a daily teaspoon of raw honey. This honey treatment continues even after the allergy is under control.*"

This form of natural immunity is made possible by the traces of pollens, dust and molds found in raw honey. However, pure bee pollen is more concentrated and contains a very potent power in causing self-immunity against allergies. Therefore, while raw honey is excellent, pollen should also be taken regularly as a highly concentrated source of self-immunization.

If you have an allergy, you are tested by your doctor to discover the cause. Once the doctor finds out the reason you are sensitive or determines the substance responsible for giving you such symptoms as chills, itching, sniffles, etc., then he will inject that particular offender in minute amounts into your bloodstream. This builds up resistance to the offender. Sometimes, this calls for lifetime injections. Often, too, there are side effects felt from these injections.

Writing in *Bee Pollen, Miracle Food*, Felix Murat says:

In France—and this is a practice that originated in the United States—doctors inject an extract from pollen to immunize the allergic person.

A doctor at the Broussais Hospital published the results obtained by this method, which so far was the best treatment known against allergies and especially against its gravest form of bronchial asthma where antihistamine and the other usual treatments did not help.

The treatment consists of repeated injections from Febru-

ary 15 to July 15, starting with two injections weekly and ending with one.

The only inconvenience of this method is that at times and on certain individuals it provokes violent reactions. It is absolutely indispensable that the injections are administered by a doctor, and the doctor must closely supervise the state of his patient for at least one hour after the injection.

The trouble, however, is that most ill persons are impatient, they think that the trouble will disappear overnight. They forget that these innumerable problems (allergies) took a long time to develop to the point of becoming noticeable; it will take time to bring them under control.

D. S. Jarvis, M.D., writing in *Folk Medicine*, says, "If honeycomb cappings (which are prime sources of pollen) are chewed once each day for one month before the expected hay fever date, the hay fever will not appear or will be mild in character."

Writing in the *American Bee Journal* (December 1950), Dr. Jarvis extols the benefits of propolis or bee glue (a constituent of comb honey) which he says "has a special action on the breathing tract . . . it opens the nose, produces a drying effect . . . lessens catarrhal discharge and . . . cough. It is for this . . . effect and the sedative effect on the body as a whole that comb honey with its propolis is used."

For more concentrated pollen there is, as mentioned earlier, pure bee pollen available in tablet or powder form at almost all health stores and many pharmacies, too, which can be taken throughout the year, on a daily basis to help the body build its own immunity to allergic distress.

Source of Youth, Vitality, Longevity.

This is the label bestowed on bee pollen by Dr. Felix Murat, who cites these additional benefits from the miracle food from the hive:

> *Combatting allergic miseries is only a minor contribution of bee pollen in comparison to its other benefits. Pollen enhances metabolism by creating endless chain reactions in the system.*
>
> *The natural minerals and other natural elements in pollen, acting as catalysts are responsible for the assimilation of nutrients in food which might otherwise be eliminated, especially in the case of processed foods.*
>
> *Processed foods lack the enzymes, natural minerals and other elements and factors, known and unknown, found in pollen. The result is that most people are overfed, undernourished and sick. There is hardly one man, woman or child not troubled with some kind of health problem, allergic or otherwise, minor or serious, diagnosed or yet undetected, due to these overprocessed foods and the polluted environment in which they are grown. . . .*
>
> *A pollen regimen will give you health, vigor, dynamism and a happy disposition, which modern living, in a very insidious way, is depriving us. Just as people go on diets of grapefruits, vegetable and fruit juices, etc., why not try one of pollen, thus introducing into your system this natural substance, overflowing with natural vitamins, minerals, proteins and so many other noble elements indispensable for your health.*[16]

❖ How Pollen Rebuilds Your Immune System

Theoretically, a certain portion of the eaten bee pollen does not go through the process of digestion. This portion remains unchanged since it is speedily assimilated into your bloodstream.

Because the membrane enclosing each pollen grain is tough, it protects the grain, sustains it and keeps it alive for weeks or even months; eating bee pollen daily will build up this supply of membrane-protected pollen in the bloodstream. And even if you breathe in windborne pollen, the reaction will be less irritating because of an improved immune system.

Eating bee pollen is similar to being injected with chemicalized or synthetic pollen by a doctor. The difference is that you nourish your body with *natural* bee pollen, strengthen your *natural* immunity, whereas with chemicals, there are risks of side effects. There is also a need for year-after-year chemical immunization. But with natural bee pollen, you avoid the inconvenience of injections; your body is not subjected to double trouble of chemicals and windborne pollen. Natural bee pollen helps strengthen your nasal and respiratory passages and boost immunity to offensive pollen.

Bodog F. Beck, M.D., author of *Honey and Your Health*, says his attention

> has been repeatedly called to the beneficial effect of honey on hay fever victims. There are many reports that the consumption of honey collected by bees from goldenrod and

fireweed will cure hay fever superinduced by the self-same pollen.

Now comes Dr. George D. McGrew of the Army Medical Corps of the William Beaumont General Hospital in El Paso, Texas, with a statement that during the hay fever season, thirty-three hay fever sufferers obtained partial or complete relief through the consumption of honey, produced in their vicinity.

The brood cells contain a considerable amount of bee bread (pollen) stored by the bees for their young. When this is orally administered it will produce a gradual immunity against the allergic symptoms caused by the same pollen.

Dr. McGrew found particular relief for patients when they chewed the honey with the wax of the brood cells. The hospital staff made an alcoholic extract from pollen and administered it in from one- to ten-drop doses, according to the requirements of the patients.[17]

So we see that pollen is a prime source of a unique type of protein which elevates the gamma globulins of the body. This process helps your body build natural immunity defense reactions to shield you against allergic distress, among other assaults on your body.

❖ How Bee Pollen Helps You Live Longer

G. Liebold, M.D., a holistic physician of Karlsruhe, Germany, author of *Bee Pollen: Valuable Food Nutriment And Remedy*, explains how bee pollen helps protect against the aging process:

> Bee pollen should be used as prophylaxis and thera-
> peutical treatment against all the disease of modern civili-
> zation. The people of today often consume too many
> calories, without getting a sufficient amount of the vital
> subtances.
>
> First in the spotlight is the need to improve the general
> condition of the body affected by nutrient malnutrition, stress
> and other negative influences.
>
> Bee pollen is an excellent prophylaxis and therapeutical
> treatment against all the precocious symptoms of old age. It
> should be considered a universal geriatric treatment in the
> form of a natural remedy.
>
> Bee pollen causes an increase in physical and mental
> abilities, especially of concentration and memory ability, ac-
> tivates sluggish metabolic functions, and strengthens the car-
> diovascular and respiratory systems.
>
> This natural nutriment from the bees removes the causes
> of cardiovascular symptoms, such as arteriosclerosis, cere-
> bral insufficiency and cellular problems. It prevents nutrient
> deficiency during old age; it is also useful for women who
> are pregnant and/or nursing.
>
> Bee pollen accelerates convalescence after serious illness
> and/or an operation, increases the body's physical defensive
> powers of the immune system, stimulates mental and psycho-
> logical resistance to stress, and creates a harmonizing of
> vegetative and hormonal disorders.
>
> Bee pollen is very complex in composition. It contains
> nutrients and vital substances in such manifold content that

this composition is unique in nature. Only the natural completeness of bee pollen explains its effectiveness.[18]

Yes, bee pollen is not only for bees—it is the most perfect food made by nature that may give you that extra edge to living a longer and healthier life.

PART THREE

Propolis

❖ Propolis—Miracle Healer from the Beehive

Bee propolis is a major breakthrough in the quest for an all-natural medicine that not only can help battle the ravages of viruses but can soothe and heal stomach ulcers. It is a remarkable antibiotic that helps nip disease reactions in the bud. It helps control runaway cell breakdown, a condition symptomatic of cancer. Health practitioners recognize it as a powerful all-natural antibiotic that can overcome disorders ranging from the common cold to arthritis to radiation injury. It is more than a miracle antibiotic and healer. It is also a source of almost all known nutrients, a "total food" with unlimited healing potential.

Just what is bee propolis? How is it prepared? How can it help you? Let us take a closer look at this powerful product.

A Sensible Look at Propolis.

Varro E. Tyler, Ph.D., dean of the School of Pharmacy at Purdue University, author of *The New Honest Herbal*, offers this clear view:

> Unlike pollen, of relatively recent medicinal use, propolis or bee glue was an official drug in the London pharmacopeias of the 17th century. However, there was a long hiatus in its popularity between the 17th and the late 20th century; now propolis once again is receiving considerable attention from laymen and scientists both. The unusual drug is of a brownish resinous material collected by bees from the buds of various poplar and conifer trees and used by the insects to fill cracks or gaps in their hives.
>
> Those who advocate its therapeutic use claim that propolis has an antibacterial activity greater than that of penicillin and other common antibiotic drugs. They maintain the product 'works' by raising the body's natural resistance to infection through stimulation of the immune system.
>
> Propolis is supposed to be especially beneficial in the treatment of tuberculosis. Duodenal ulcers and gastric disturbances are also thought to benefit from propolis therapy. Applied externally in the form of a cream, advocates say it relieves various types of dermatitis, especially those caused

by bacteria and fungi. *Propolis is commercially available in the form of capsules (both pure and combined with 50% pollen), throat lozenges, cream, chips (used like chewing gum), and as a powder (to prepare a tincture.)*

More than 25 different constituents of propolis have now been tested scientifically against various species of bacteria and fungi for antibacterial and antifungal effects. . . .

A series of studies on propolis carried out in recent years by Polish investigators showed that besides bacteriostatic and fungistatic properties, the drug inhibited the growth of protozoa, accelerated bone formation, had regenerative effects on tissues, stimulated some enzyme action, and showed cytostatic effects (inhibited cell growth and division).

It must be emphasized that all of these results were obtained from experiments carried out in vitro, that is, in the chemical laboratory outside the living body, or in small animals.

The flavonoid pigments of propolis seem to possess modest antibacterial and antifungal properties but much less active than the standard drugs for controlling such microorganisms. Other tentative claims for potential therapeutic utility require clinical verification.[19]

❖ Protects Against Bacterial Infections

James Balch, M.D., a Fellow of the American College of Surgeons from Greenfield, Indiana and author of *Prescription for Natural Healing*, states

Propolis is a resinous substance collected from various plants by bees; it is not made by bees. It is used together with beeswax in the construction of hives.

As a supplement, it is an excellent aid against bacterial infections. A Soviet scientist stated that bee propolis stimulates phagocytosis, which helps the white blood cells to destroy bacteria. Soviet surgeons often feed honey to their patients before surgery as a precaution against infection. . . .

Bee propolis is also good as a salve and for abrasions and bruises because of its antibacterial effect. Reports proclaim good results against inflammation of the mucous membranes of the mouth and throat, dry cough and throat, halitosis, tonsillitis, ulcers, and acne, and for the stimulation of the immune system. . . .

Be sure that all products from the bee are fresh and tightly sealed. It is best to purchase these products from a manufacturer who specializes in bee products. When used for allergies, it is best to obtain bee products that are produced within a ten-mile radius. This way, those with allergies get a minute dose of pollen to desensitize them to the local pollen in the area.[20]

❖ Getting Acquainted with Bee Propolis

Bee propolis is a resinous material, gathered by bees from the leaf buds and bark of trees, especially poplars and firs. This substance has been around for at least 45 million years, and has recently been "rediscovered" for its healing properties.

The name "propolis" is derived from the Greek *pro* (before) and *polis* (city), so named because in its natural state, bees use propolis to prevent entrance to their "wax city" and keep out harmful intruders.

Propolis begins with a sticky substance from deciduous and conifer trees. The bees use this propolis to seal up any holes or cracks in the hives. Propolis is also used to fix the roof of the hive. It is a natural form of "cement" or "building material" that provides protection to the bees from outside contaminants while these residents remain in the hive.

Self-protective Uses.

For the hive, propolis is a multiple source of protection. Bees use propolis to glue down loose parts of the hive to protect it from cold and rain. They use it as a barrier against their enemies (other bees, antagonistic insects or rodents) by making labyrinthine entrances into the hive so that only a few bees are needed to guard it.

Bees also coat propolis on the entire surface of the hive, polishing it so that at the same time it protects their wings from sharp outcroppings.

Propolis Before Eggs.

Before the queen lays her eggs in the cell, the bees clean it out. They line this cleansed cell with a fine, almost microscopic coating of propolis. Only then will the queen lay her eggs in what has become an absolutely sterile environment.

The beehive has proven over and over to be the most sterile environment in the animal kingdom. With nearly 100,000 bees per hive, there is very little bacteria because of propolis. It acts as a natural antibiotic, killing infections. It is this type of environment that can cleanse the human organism and combat the threat of infection.

Serves Two Purposes for Hive.

Propolis is a sealant and tightener for the hive. It protects the bee from bacterial and viral infections. Secondly, when the resinous propolis solidifies in the cracks and openings of the hive, it acts to control the internal environment while reinforcing and protecting the hive from intruders. The entrance to the hive would be the easiest way for infection to enter the colony if it were not for propolis. Placed behind the entryway so that all entering bees must cross over it, propolis protects the hive's inhabitants from infection.

Natural Penicillin Action.

Can propolis be considered a form of natural penicillin? To understand how propolis can be a natural antibiotic, note the following: if a rodent enters the hive and it is stung to death, it remains in the hive since the bees cannot move the heavy foreign invader. To prevent decay, the bees encase the rodent in propolis, then wrap beeswax around the entire mass. Thus embalmed, the rodent body remains intact without any decay or decomposition for at least five years.

This same principle is studied by scientists as a means of

immobilizing infectious bacteria and viruses. That is, using propolis to surround the infectious agent, seal it up and render it useless. In the human organism, the propolis-wrapped virus can be destroyed and eliminated. And unlike penicillin or other drugs, propolis is always effective because bacteria and viruses cannot build tolerance against it.

So we see that the beehive is a miniature city teeming with life. The temperature inside the hive is kept at approximately 95°F. with 90% humidity—a perfect breeding ground for all kinds of molds, mildews and bacteria. Yet the hive remains the most sterile environment found in nature. The bee is the only insect to have been found free of bacteria. Reason: propolis has antibacterial and fungicidal agents and contains many different antibiotic substances.

And it all ties in with the source of propolis—the poplar and fir trees. When a tree is damaged, it secretes a sap-like resin which covers the wound and protects the tree from invading micro-organisms. The bees gather this resin and improve it by adding enzymes, pollen and wax. It is transported by the bees in "baskets" on their hind legs, mixed with a secretion, and subsequently used in the hive to repair cracks and openings.

❖ Healer Used by the Ancients

This powerful healer has been used to treat wounds and so-called "incurable" ailments for hundreds of centuries.

Hippocrates (a Greek physician, c.460–c.377 B.C., considered the father of medicine) prescribed the use of this resinous substance to help heal sores and ulcers, both external and internal.

Propolis-making bees were depicted on vases from ancient Egypt where the sign of the bee was often interwoven with the titles of the kings and used as the motif on ornaments presented as rewards for valor. The ancient Egyptians used bee propolis to help correct many ailments.

Legend has it that Jupiter (chief god in Roman mythology) transformed the beautiful Melissa into a bee so that she could prepare this miracle substance for use in healing.

Roman Recognition.

In his massive *Natural History,* Pliny, the Roman scholar (A.D. 23–79) offers much on the use of resins such as propolis. Pliny writes that "current physicians use propolis as a medicine because it extracts stings and all substances embedded in the flesh, reduces swelling, softens indurations [hardened tissue], soothes pains of the sinews and heals sores when it appears hopeless for them to mend."

Pliny describes how the bees would use propolis as a disinfectant for brood cells and the interior of the hive; also a mixture of propolis and wax would close holes and reinforce structurally weak areas. Mention is also made how propolis was used to reduce the size of the entrance to the bees' *polis* or city. Pliny identifies the medicinal action of propolis, explaining how it reduces swellings, soothes pain and heals many sores.

It has been established that bees are impervious to any virus or bacteria. This innate ability to defend themselves against infectious disease is very important. Any contagion could run rampant and rapidly destroy as many as 100,000 members of a colony living together in the very close quarters of the hive. Certainly the bees' good health can be attributed, at least in part, to a genetic immunity.

Bees are out and about in an increasingly polluted environment every day. They come in contact with many chemicals, some that could be destructive in a short time. Yet, they have this strong natural protection. Experts point out that the bees are "decontaminated" as they pass over the propolis barrier guarding the entrance.

Europeans Discover Propolis.

John Gerard's famous herbal work, *The Historie of Plants* (1597, Great Britain) refers to "the resin or clammy substance of the black poplar tree buds" which can provide swift and effective healing for many conditions. Apothecaries of this era would use propolis as a major ingredient in healing ointments.

Soothes Inflammation.

Nicholas Culpeper's famous 17th-century *Complete Herbal*, under the heading of "The Poplar Tree" tells us that "the ointment called propolis is singularly good for all heat [fever] and inflammations in many parts of the body and cools the heat of the wounds."

In Green's *Universal Herbal* (1824) under *Populus Nigra* (Black Poplar Tree), it is said that "the young leaves are an excellent ingredient for poultices for hard and painful swellings. The buds of both this and the White Poplar smell very pleasant in the spring. Being pressed between the fingers, they yield a balsamic resinous substance which smells like storax." Says Green, "A drachm of this tincture in broth is administered in internal ulcers and excoriations [external skin lesions] and is said to have removed obstinate or abnormal discharges from the intestines."

❖ Propolis: What's in It for You

So we see that propolis is composed of a resinous substance collected by bees from the buds, leafy stalks and young twigs of certain trees. Propolis comes from the sap or juice secreted by trees which fights their own infection and disease and heals cuts. Just what does propolis contain to make it such a powerful healer?

Danish scientist Dr. K. Lund Aagaard, author of a paper, "Propolis, Natural Substance: The Way to Health," considered an expert on the use of this healer, tells us the following:

> Propolis is one of the most efficient bee products from the viewpoint of active principles transmitted from plant to man. Its main sources are the substances collected from poplar or Salicineae buds. The bees add salivary secretions and wax to the resinous raw substance.
>
> Nineteen substances of different chemical structure have been identified so far. For instance, there are those from the group of so-called flavonoids, betulene and betulenol, isovanillin, resins, aromatic unsaturated acids—caffeic and ferulic, characterized by biological activity.

It must be noted that, in general, the prevalence of the poplar being maintained—the source of the vegetable raw material used by the bees in preparing propolis is very varied. However, the permanent chemical substances, respectively the active principles contained both in propolis and in the exudation of buds and bark are almost identical. Only the proportions may differ from one source species to another.

During my long practice, I had the opportunity to examine many afflictions and often experimented with propolis in its natural form. I obtained relevant results for the cases treated. Based on close cooperation, these experiments involved more than 50,000 persons all across Scandinavia.

The field of influence of propolis is extremely broad and includes: swelling of the large intestine, catarrh of the eyes, infection of the urinary tract, swelling of the throat, gout, open wounds, sinus swellings, colds, influenza, bronchitis, gastritis, cancer, diseases of the ears, periodontial disease, intestinal infections, ulcers, eczema eruptions, pneumonia, arthritis, lung disease, stomach virus, headaches, Parkinson's disease, bile infections, sclerosis, circulation deficiencies, warts, conjunctivitis and hoarseness.

Propolis has a refreshing effect both for regulating hormones and as an antibiotic substance which is in itself a stimulator of the natural resistance of the body. Propolis may be used by everybody, sick or healthy, as a means of protection against microorganisms. Propolis is also efficient in a series of disorders caused by bacteria, viruses or different fungi. Propolis cures almost all diseases because it is a special natural substance.

The whole research program, with thousands of cases,

had a single purpose, namely, to obtain a substance with the greatest efficiency against the greatest number of diseases mentioned. The numerous healings are relevant by themselves and the number of people who use propolis is ever increasing.[21]

What Is in Propolis?

Propolis contains approximately 55 percent resins and balms, 30 percent wax, 10 percent etheric oils and 5 percent pollen. These basic ingredients have dynamic bacteria-destroying power. They do this flawlessly, yet they render no adverse side effects. Unlike chemical medicines such as penicillin which can produce reactions, propolis will not cause such upset. This has been clinically verified after its use in more than 16,000 situations.[21]

It is believed to be rich in amino acids, composite ethers of univalent alcohols and trace elements including iron, copper, manganese, zinc and antibiotics. It has a high vitamin content, especially the valuable bioflavonoids.

Propolis is usually chestnut or greenish-brown in color. It gives off a pleasant aroma of poplar buds, honey and vanilla.

❖ The Bioflavonoid Connection

As a natural therapeutic, propolis power may well be attributed to its rich concentration of bioflavonoids (a group of nutrients that enhance the effectiveness of vitamin C). Bioflavonoids are recognized as being able to heal the capillary system, mend the fragility and permeability of the blood vessels; act as a vasodilator and diuretic, and are recognized as vital to build the immune system to fight disease. In medical circles, bioflavonoids are often referred to as vitamin P.

Importance of Bioflavoids.

The late naturopathic physician, Dr. Paavo Airola of Phoenix, Arizona, emphasized their value:

> During the past thirty years, many research projects and clinical investigations have been undertaken on the prophylactic and therapeutic properties of the bioflavonoids.
>
> Over five hundred scientific papers on bioflavonoids have been published in reputable medical journals around the world. Clinical reports have shown that bioflavonoid therapy is effective in such diversified conditions as rheumatic fever, spontaneous abortions and miscarriages, high blood pressure, respiratory infections, hemorrhoids, cirrhosis of the liver, etc.[22]

And propolis is a powerhouse of this all-healing nutrient!

European healing circles are abuzz with the power of propolis (chiefly because of its bioflavonoid concentration) as a virus fighter. In an exclusive interview with Bent Havsteen, M.D., formerly of Cornell University and now with Kiel University in Germany, these discoveries were revealed:

"Bioflavonoids in propolis have a protective effect on virus infections. Let me explain. Viruses are enclosed in a protein coat. As long as the coat remains unbroken, the infectious and dangerous material remains imprisoned and is harmless to the organism. We have found that an enzyme which normally removes the protein coat is being inhibited; thus, dangerous viral material is kept locked in. The protein coating around the virus is maintained by the flavonoids in propolis; these flavonoids keep the virus inactive. It is the same as being immune to the virus, but only with the presence of bioflavonoids as in propolis."

Dr. Bent Havsteen says that propolis offers these valuable healing responses, thanks to the bioflavonoids.

Sore throats:

"This is due to inflammation and infection in mucous membranes. Symptoms such as pain and increased body temperature are common. These symptoms are caused by fat compounds called prostaglandins. The bioflavonoids in propolis actually block the building of these prostaglandins. It is like building immunity to sore throats and related ailments."

All natural "aspirin."

Dr. Havsteen explains, "The action of propolis bioflavonoids is almost identical with that of aspirin. They block the same enzyme. But propolis has an advantage over aspirin because it has no side effects. We call it a natural aspirin."

Dr. Havsteen adds that propolis bioflavonoids inhibit or block those enzymes that produce the prostaglandins which cause pain and fever. Symptoms disappear after a small amount of propolis, as has been reported in many cases.

Stimulates Interferon Production.

Interferon is a natural protein substance able to fight many diseases. Dr. Havsteen explains that propolis bioflavonoids do, in fact, stimulate body production of this natural immune booster. "The bioflavonoids stimulate the white blood cells or lymphocytes, to produce interferon. And with this substance in the body, there is tremendous resistance to many infections."

Soothes Allergies.

Propolis is also a prime source of histamine and serotonin, two substances needed by the body to help cope with allergies. But when something goes wrong, an excess pours out which triggers allergic reactions. It is like having too much of a good thing. Dr. Havsteen explains:

> Histamine and serotonin are tissue hormones. They remain in the mast cells. But when an allergen binds itself to the outside of the cell, these two substances leak out and cause an allergic reaction. The trick is to block the leakage of these substances. We have found this can be done with the use of the bioflavonoids in propolis. They block the acids that would break into the cells and cause release of the allergy-causing substances. Again, we see that propolis can create this form of built-in immunity.

Periodontal Problems.

One of the leading causes of dental problems is the erosion of the gums and tissues that line the pockets of the mouth in which teeth are secured. Inflammation and infectious bleeding may cause weakening of the bone structure and tooth loss. Dr. Havsteen suggests the use of propolis because the bioflavonoids

> block the formation of the prostaglandins which cause decomposition. In that way, bleeding is diminished. But there is another benefit. The bioflavonoids stimulate enzyme formation to fortify the walls of the blood vessels in the gums. In this way, we have a two-pronged or multi-pronged attack on the diseased areas of the mouth. I suggest that gum-troubled people use propolis daily. I advise some to chew propolis lozenges.[23]

So we see that the action of propolis bioflavonoids is a way of boosting inner immunity for many ailments. And this is the tip of the iceberg. Still more miracle healings have been announced.

❖ Healings Reported with Propolis

Scientists from all parts of the world report that dynamic healing is possible with supervised administration of propolis.

Some amazing announcements were reported to the *American Chiropractor:*

Irradiation Disease.

At the Institute of Radiology in Sarajevo, Yugoslavia, a team of physicians treated patients suffering from irradiation complications, diagnosed as irradiation diseases.

These patients had serious liver damage caused by improper protein metabolism, as well as from the effects of X and Y rays. Over a period of two months, these patients were given propolis. A double-blind test was made by giving a placebo (dummy pill) to another set of patients with irradiation disease. The doctors report that those who took propolis were healed by its biological substances so the radiation problems "lessened or disappeared." No improvements could be observed in the control group given the placebo.[24]

High Blood Fat.

Dr. Fang Chu of the Workers' Hospital in the Kiangsu Province in the People's Republic of China, told of giving propolis to patients who had hyperlipidemia, or high blood fat. The forty-five patients also had problems with hypertension, arteriosclerosis and coronary heart disease. Dr. Chu gave the patients 0.3 grams of propolis by oral administration, three times daily for four weeks. "Clinical results suggest that there was a lowering of hyperlipidemia as well as propolis' effect during the treatment of arteriosclerosis or coronary heart disease."[24]

Ulcers.

Dr. Franz Klemens Feiks of Austria tells of using a five percent extract of propolis in the treatment of ulcers. "We give a dose of five drops in water before meals, three times a day. The group taking propolis showed pain disappeared after three days in seven out of ten cases. After ten days, no wounds could be detected in six out of the ten patients taking the propolis." So we see that, according to Dr. Feiks, the use of propolis not only helps diminish and even end ulcers, but promotes internal healing of such sores and wounds.

Herpes Zoster.

In this condition, there is a skin eruption such as shingles. A virus-caused condition, it is basically a disease of the nerves. Skin lesions appear along the sites supplied by the infected nerve centers. The first symptom is usually a crop of small blisters accompanied by pain. Dr. Franz Feiks says he gave such patients a "five percent solution of the propolis, once a day. In all of the twenty-one cases I treated, pain disappeared within forty-eight hours and did not reappear. In three cases, only itching persisted over a long period of time. Application of the propolis extract in the form of a spray from an atomizer did not work. We applied it locally with a brush."[24]

Women's Friend.

Propolis has been effective in easing gynecological or female disorders. In particular, three doctors from the clinic for obstetrics and gynecology at the Crimean Medical Institute tell of using propolis as a salve.

The doctors treated women who had erosion of the neck of the uterus, irritated cervix, cellular disorder and vaginal problems. They applied a solution of propolis salve, right on the eroded surface. Within four to five days, some healing was noted. Complete recovery was reported by the end of twelve days, attributed to *daily* application of propolis salve. A few women did not respond; this is not unusual since each person is different. But propolis salve was seen to be curative in almost 98 percent of the cases.

"In cases of vaginal and uterine neck inflammation, the application of propolis brings about the local disappearance of the symptoms of trychomonadosis," reports Henryk Suchy, M.D., a Polish gynecologist. Special propolis tablets were used in healing these women. Dr. Suchy reports, "Disappearance of symptoms and uterine neck inflammation was also observed after local applications of thirty milligrams propolis vaginal tablets."

Other gynecologists in Poland tell of treating female students troubled with dysmenorrhea (painful menstruation) by using propolis successfully to soothe pain in fifty out of sixty women. Say these scientists, "The propolis salve has no toxic properties or irritant reaction. It quickly stimulates the epithelialization of the affected area." Itching, dryness, hemorrhoidal distress were also some problems speedily healed with bee propolis salve."[24]

New Hope for Cancer Control.

Mitja Vösnjak, former Deputy Minister of Foreign Affairs of Yugoslavia, tells of a patient, Rudy, who was wasting away from cancer.

Someone brought in a bottle of propolis in liquid form. The attending physician prescribed ten or fifteen drops in a little water, half an hour before meals, three times a day. That was all the cancer-troubled Rudy was to take. Within a few days, the former deputy tells of talking to Rudy who

113

said, "No pains, no cramps, no blood. If it's true, it'll be a real miracle."

After six weeks, Rudy ate better and started to gain needed weight. He had "healthy pink cheeks, the old enthusiastic, self-confident look in his eyes, decisive movements and quick firm footsteps. Above all, he overflowed with plans and ideas, had great hopes that he would be able to work again, to catch up on the past seven years and wipe them from his life as if they had never existed."

Propolis is credited with helping turn the tide and bringing cancer under control so that Rudy would have a second chance for a healthy life.[25]

❖ The Doctors Praise Healing Power of Propolis

According to Roy Kupsinel, M.D., of Maitland, Florida, propolis is chock-full of healing power.

> *I prescribe propolis for many of my patients as a safe nutritional supplement. When taken regularly, it actually creates an antibiotic disease-fighting reaction to almost any illness—without dangerous side effects.*
>
> *The bees have relied upon propolis for 46 million years. They must be doing something right because beehives contain less bacteria and are more sterile than hospitals! Propolis— it's incredible!*[26]

Source of Life Energy.

John Diamond, M.D., President of the International Academy of Preventive Medicine, tells of seeing many remarkable benefits due to propolis:

> *Of all the natural supplements I have tested, the one that seems to be the most strengthening to the thymus, and hence the life energy, is bee resin, or bee propolis, a resin secreted by trees and then metabolized by the bees, which bring it back to the hive to line the interior.*
>
> *This substance is the subject of considerable clinical research in several European countries. For many years, it has proved to be effective against bacteria, viruses and fungi. We now know that the reason for this is that propolis activates the thymus gland and therefore the immune system.*
>
> *Our life energy is the source of our physical and mental wellbeing, of glowing health, of the joy of living . . . unfortunately 95 percent of the general population tests low on the life energy scale.*
>
> *I have never seen a patient with a chronic degenerative illness who did not have an underactive thymus gland . . . I believe it is the thymus weakness, or underactivity, that is the original cause of the illness.*[27]

By activating the thymus gland, propolis can help keep a body in good health. It helps stimulate the body's immune response. Scientists recognize the importance of having a strong thymus gland. Found in the root of the neck, it consists largely of lymphocytes, the white blood cells needed to boost immunity against infection and illness.

Antibacterial Power.

Noted USSR scientist V. P. Kivalkina, reporting to *Antibiotics*, describes tests used to confirm the bacteria-fighting power of propolis. He tells of testing 28 different types of propolis from the various regions and republics of the former USSR, Bulgaria and Czechoslovakia. Dr. Kivalkina says that bee propolis, however gathered, has such self-activating power, it sustains its anti-bacterial characteristics even if stored for many years under proper conditions."[28]

Cleanses Cells, Bloodstream.

European scientist V. A. Balalykin reports that bee propolis has cell-blood cleansing and revitalizing values, and the ability to sweep away harmful bacteria. In tests, the doctor notes that propolis stimulates the reaction of phagocytosis. That is, alerting the white blood cells to engulf and digest bacteria and wastes. This detoxifies them out of the bloodstream. It creates a self-cleansing action. Essentially, bee propolis initiates an accelerated intracellular digestion of staphylococci (poison-forming substances) and promotes a cleansing of cells and bloodstream. It stimulates a major healing reaction.[29]

Fights Flu.

Scientist N. P. Iojris of the former USSR reports that propolis has unique flu fighting powers. Flu or influenza is a virus infection, primarily of the respiratory passages; it has effects on the body and can cause fever, headache, weakness. The virus can be dangerous; the special risk is increased bacterial infection of the lungs.

Dr. Iojris tells of tests in which an alcohol extract of propolis was found to boost a preventive benefit not only for the flu but other virus diseases.[30]

Overcomes Virus Infections.

An explanation was offered by Soviet scientist, K. A. Kuzmina, who delivered a paper showing that propolis has a toning and fortifying effect on the body. Under the influence of propolis, the virus-fighting power of phagocytosis is strengthened. The content of the protective virus-fighting protein, properdin, starts to rise in the blood. There is a speeding of the detoxification power of certain antibodies.[31]

Treats Gastrointestinal Disorders.

Stomach and duodenum (first section of the intestine) disorders respond favorably to the presence of propolis. The gastrointestinal tract falls victim to such ailments as an ulcer or an abscess. Russian scientists note that propolis is able to promote resistance to ulcer formation; and hasten recovery if an ulcer is present.

Dr. F. D. Makarov reports on tests in which he treated various patients suffering from gastrointestinal disorders. Symptoms included nausea, heartburn, poor appetite; also both hyperacidity and hypoacidity (too much or too little acid). The doctor prescribed propolis—specifically, twenty drops to be taken three times a day. After three to five days, all patients were relieved of pain. Acidity became normalized. Nausea and heartburn stopped entirely. Even problems of enlarged liver were relieved as this master body organ resumed its normal size. The abscess or ulcer was also healed. All this was seen to happen within ten to twelve days, at the most. The *daily* use of propolis stimulated this all-natural healing of stomach disorders.

This statement was issued by the scientist:

> *On the basis of the facts cited from the literature, we can draw the conclusion that bee propolis is a medical preparation with bactericidal, antitoxic, antiinflammatory and anesthetising properties. In addition, it normalizes the secreting functions of the stomach. It can be recommended for the treatment of patients who are suffering from ulcers (abscesses) in the stomach and/or duodenum. Recovery occurs more quickly with treatment by propolis than it does with the use of common medicines.* [32]

Heals Skin of Youngsters.

Propolis salve, in use since 1962 at the K. A. Rachfuss Children's Hospital in St. Petersburg, is recognized for its healing powers. Patients who had infected wounds or newborns with tissue disorders were given propolis salve. Scientist Dr. G. F. Zabelina tells that propolis is able to curb inflammation and disinfect wounds. In addition, it is able to stimulate new skin growth. Dr. Zabelina recommends its use to heal infected burns. [33]

❖ Folk Remedies

Because propolis seals out bacteria from the beehive, the same principle should apply to common and uncommon disorders. The use of propolis immobilizes infectious invaders and helps the body recover from various ailments. Here is a collection of reported folk remedy healers using propolis.

◆ SORE LIPS AND GUMS ◆

Put a few drops of propolis solution in a half glass of water. It will turn cloudy or milk-like in color. Drink a little in the morning, a bit more in the afternoon and the balance in the evening. It helps heal mouth sores, scratches, etc.

◆ BRUISES ◆

Combine propolis with honey. Apply this ointment to gauze and use as a bandage dressing. Wrap dressing around affected area and let remain overnight. Renew daily until bruises are healed.

◆ BURNS ◆

Put a few drops of propolis onto the affected area as a natural healing ointment. Within moments, you feel cooled. Healing comes shortly afterward.

◆ SORE THROAT ◆

Take a few drops of propolis on a slice of wholegrain bread. Eat it as a natural antibiotic. Helps fight the microbes and viruses responsible for respiratory distress.

◆ NATURAL ANTIBIOTIC ◆

For any health problem requiring an antibiotic, try natural propolis. The advantage is that you are safe with propolis which is a "natural medicine" and "natural antibiotic." Your body may be allergic to chemotherapeutic medicines which may cause undesirable reactions. Propolis can also cool feverish inflammations.

◆ SKIN BLEMISHES ◆

Soak propolis onto a small pad of cotton or gauze. Smear over facial spots such as acne, pimples, etc. Repeat as often as possible, especially after washing. Helpful if left on overnight. Clears up blemishes within a short time.

◆ NASAL CONGESTION ◆

Take a few drops of propolis in a tepid liquid at least three times daily. Helps decrease nasal secretions, clear nasal infections, open up clogged respiratory passages to allow for healthier and easier breathing.

✦ RESPIRATORY DISTRESS ✦

For a scratchy throat, stubborn cough, try this remedy: combine a few drops of propolis with some honey, add to herb tea. Stir vigorously. Drink a lukewarm cup several times daily. Helps you breathe better; gives you a "smooth as silk" throat.

✦ INJURED BONES ✦

Use propolis as a tonic throughout the day. Helps hasten better knitting of the bone matrix.

❖ Propolis Preparations

When gathered from beehives, propolis is prepared in these easy-to-use forms:

Lozenges.

A sweet-tasting and effective way for soothing a sore throat, relieving a cough due to colds and related respiratory problems.

Capsules.

A concentrated extract of propolis in the form of pure soft gelatin capsules.

Tincture.

Made by liquifying propolis in a solvent such as alcohol. It is put through a cold-process vacuum distillation system that removes the solvent and leaves the propolis and its essential oils. Use as a gargle (four or five drops in half a glass of tepid water) for throat disorders.

Salve.

A tincture of propolis in a salve is soothing when applied to the skin.

Tablets.

Essentially the same as the capsules but in handy tablet form.

Granules.

Great for chewing to release full effects of this healing bee product.

Powder.

Pulverized powder for easy swallowing with water or your favorite fruit or vegetable juice.

Easy to use, quick to produce healing results, propolis is recognized as nature's remarkable healing gift to mankind.

Utilized in different ways, it is a protective device for the entire bee kingdom. Transferred into the human equation, it becomes a powerful natural healer to resist the rigors and stresses customarily afflicting mankind.

So we see that propolis is a specific for everything from inflammation of the gums to fatigue and tiredness. Taken from the resins of selected trees, propolis is considered a substance vital to the perpetuation of the marvelous bee. It is needed for the bee's continued life as a colony. Propolis becomes a protective defense against invading enemies. Modern scientists have isolated it, used it in thousands of situations the world over, and proved that propolis is a powerful healer and a dynamic antibiotic.

PART
FOUR

Royal Jelly

❖ Royal Jelly: Fountain of Youth

Royal jelly is a white, milky substance produced in the glands of worker honey bees to feed the queen bee. All the larvae receive this royal jelly or bees' milk for the first three days of their lives. Afterwards, they are nourished on a diet of honey, pollen and water.

This bees' milk is a concentrated super food responsible for turning an ordinary worker bee into a long-lived reproductive dynamo—the queen bee. It is her only food. The queen bee grows 40 to 60% larger than the worker bees and lives five or more years compared to her genetically identical sister whose lifespan is only 40 days.

❖ Doctors Who Recommend Royal Jelly

James F. Balch, M.D., board certified by the American Board of Urology and a fellow in the American College of Surgeons, has this to say:

> The thick, milky substance that is secreted from the pharyngeal glands of a special group of young nurse bees between their sixth and twelfth days of life is called royal jelly.
>
> When honey and pollen are combined and refined within the young nurse bee, royal jelly is naturally created.
>
> It contains all of the B-complex vitamins including a high concentration of pantothenic acid (B5) and pyridoxine (B6), and is the only natural source of pure acetylcholine. Royal jelly also contains minerals, vitamins A, C, D and E, enzymes, hormones, eighteen amino acids, and antibacterial and antibiotic components.
>
> This product must be combined with honey to preserve its potency. Royal jelly is known to aid in bronchial asthma, liver disease, pancreatitis, insomnia, stomach ulcers, kidney disease, bone fractures, and skin disorders, and is a potentiator of the immune system. Royal jelly spoils easily. Keep it refrigerated and make sure it is tightly sealed.[34]

Dr. Alfred Vogel, author of *The Nature Doctor*, lauds this miracle food with these findings based upon his practice in natural healing:

Not everyone knows that a worker bee's busy life is over after twenty-eight working days. Or did you know that the egg cells that normally produce worker bees can, when fed with a special substance, develop into queens? There is something mysterious about this wonder of nature.

For one thing, the queens are considerably bigger than the other bees, and, what is more, they live sixty times longer. A very special nutritive fluid is collected by the workers for those cells which ultimately produce queens. Although this phenomenon has been the subject of extensive scientific investigation, the understanding of its exact nature still eludes the researchers and only some of the jelly's constituents have been isolated.

The ancients perhaps knew more about it than we do, as we frequently find references to "ambrosia," "nectar" and other wonder foods in their writings. It is not unreasonable to assume they were referring to what is now called "royal jelly."

Unfortunately, no reference as to how this ambrosia was obtained is to be found, so our assumption must remain speculative. There is no doubt, however, that royal jelly possesses biological qualities of the highest order, for it enables the queen to lay as many as 2000 eggs daily, and this with a single fertilization. This is, indeed, a marvelous biological achievement, which stands unrivalled in nature.

Scientific and popular periodicals have devoted much space to the subject of royal jelly. True, this promotion no doubt has something to do with cleverly disguised advertising, since every manufacturer believes his product to be the best on the market.

On the other hand, these efforts demonstrate that today's world needs a biologically safe natural tonic, as opposed to a chemical or synthetic one.

No one really knows how the bees manufacture the natural compound. All we can say is that the Creator gave them the necessary instinct to make this complex substance from the raw materials they have available in nature. What they produce proves the truth of the concept that food should be medicine and medicines should be food.

Some years ago the newspapers reported that the Pope had recovered from a severe illness after his personal physician had prescribed royal jelly as a tonic for him. It was also reported that Dr. Paul Niehans, an eminent endocrinologist and specialist in live-cell therapy, concluded that royal jelly vitalizes the glandular system in a similar way to an injection of fresh endocrine cells. These observations are a strong enough indication that it is indeed appropriate to pay much more attention to royal jelly in the future.

As long ago as in April, 1956, at the Second International Biogenetic Congress held in Baden-Baden, Germany, many of the papers presented dealt with the research findings in connection with royal jelly.

Then there were the articles written by Professor Belvefer of Paris, who had been conducting research on royal jelly for decades. It is amazing to read his references to the findings made by a number of researchers, for example the fact that the queen bee is able to lay 300,000-450,000 eggs a year as a result of her feeding on this remarkable nutritive *complex. This feat cannot be matched by any other creature on earth.*

Further reports explained that royal jelly not only vitalizes and rejuvenates through its efforts on the endocrine glands, but also successfully combats whooping cough and asthma, especially in children. It has been found that children with a weak constitution soon pick up and have better appetites when given royal jelly.

Benefits can also be obtained in cases of bronchitis, migraine, stomach and gallbladder troubles, digestive disorders, bad nerves and the peculiar kind of fatigue resulting from weak functioning of the endocrine glands. These and many other health problems can be improved considerably, if not cured, by taking royal jelly regularly.

Moreover, it is maintained that people with a predisposition to cancer will benefit from a regular intake of royal jelly. It is also good for the skin when taken orally and when used for massage. For the latter, dilute some royal jelly with honey and water and massage the solution into the skin.[35]

❖ The Miracle of Royal Jelly and the Queen Bee

So we see that royal jelly is the rich royal milk fed to the queen bee for her entire life. It is mandatory in the making of a queen. Yes, queen bees are made, not born!

Eggs to be reared as queens are placed in specially prepared super-size brood cells. The eggs deposited therein by the queen mother are identical to those eggs which are destined to become the sexless worker bees of the hive.

Royden Brown, who has devoted decades to the study of the bees and their health producing products, author of *How to Live the Millenium*, tells us how a queen bee is made and why royal jelly is such a powerful healer from the hive.

The Rearing of Worker Bees.

During the first three days of larval development, the baby worker bees are fed a diluted form of royal jelly liberally mixed with honey. This rich brood food is supplied so generously that the tiny young larvae actually lie in a pool of it within their individual brood comb cells. But this mass feeding period comes abruptly to an end after three days. The quality of the brood food changes. Quantities are reduced sharply.

During the last three days of larval life, less rich food is supplied. It is given only as it is needed. During the final stages, the development of the worker-larva's sex glands is suppressed. But the development of brood food glands, the glands which will secrete royal jelly to feed the queen, mature. The wax glands develop fully. Should royal jelly, even in diluted form, continue to be supplied, a queen would be produced.

The Rearing of a Queen.

Throughout her entire larval period, an egg reared to be queen is supplied with highly-nutritive hormone-rich royal jelly. Without this rich royal milk, she would fail to develop

132

properly and the result would be merely another worker for the hive. It is this royal diet which single-handedly transforms her into a queen.

The Queen Bee and Her Power.

As she continues to feed on royal jelly past the three day cut-off for workers, the queen grows a modified stinger. Unlike worker bees, the queen's stinger is curved, not straight.

The "queen's guard" takes care of hive defense, so she will never sting an intruder or give her life to protect the entrance to the hive. Because the queen will use her stinger only to defend her royal right to rule, the queen can retract her stinger after shooting out venom. Unlike a worker bee, the queen does not die after stinging.

Differences in Bees.

There are other major differences in the development process, too. As an adult, the queen will have no wax glands. It is the worker bees who build the comb. The queen will have no pollen baskets on her back legs. It is the workers who forage for pollen and propolis. And the queen will have no hypopharyngeal glands to secrete royal jelly. Nurse bees secrete royal jelly.

The Queen Develops.

The queen's sex organs progress to fully-ripe maturity as she passes through the larval and pupal stages of her development. When she emerges as a royal adult queen, her body will be noticeably larger and clearly superior to those of her sisters, the sexless workers of the hive. (An average queen bee measures 17 mm. and weighs 200 mg. compared to 12 mm. and 125 mg. for the worker bee. Royal jelly gives the royal beauty a 42 percent increase in size and a 60 percent superiority in weight over the workers of the court.

The Advantage of the Queen.

Nature builds in yet another advantage. Because the queen is so necessary to the colony, her royal development to full adulthood is accomplished in just 16 days, thanks to her richly royal diet, compared to the 21 days it takes to rear a worker.

The queen has another advantage, too. Her lifespan is measured in years, while a worker bee's lifespan is measured in weeks. A queen will live forty times longer than the ladies of her court. In the wild, a queen will live productively for five to seven years. Worker bees become worn out and die at an average age of seven to eight weeks. Workers are expendable—the queen is not.

The Power of the Queen.

During her remarkably extended lifespan, the queen will lay around 2000 eggs per day. *Each batch of brood has a total weight greater than two-and-one-half times her own body weight.* The queen feasts on royal jelly throughout her entire lifetime. This remarkable food alone insures her superior development and incredible longevity. Remember, a queen does not start off with an inborn genetic superiority. It is the direct feeding of each and every cell in her body with richly-nutritive royal jelly which first creates and then sustains the queen for the whole of her extra-long life.[36]

❖ A Closer Look at Royal Jelly

This unique substance is fed directly from the worker to the queen. Consequently, beekeepers themselves have not been able to closely examine royal jelly. But new findings have been made.

Nurse bees ranging in age from five to fifteen days secrete the rich royal milk. During the nursing phase, these workers almost force-feed themselves to the bursting point on an unbelievably rich diet of bee pollen and honey so they can produce royal jelly. The queen drinks all the creamy thick fluid she wants from a nurse's hypopharyngeal gland.

So we see that royal jelly is manufactured in the bodies of the nurse bees while they digest bee pollen—this is a major reason for its remarkable quantities of hormonal substance and the strong unique proteins found in its highly nitrogenous composition. Actually, the fragrance is rather pungent to a human nose but the queen seems to find royal jelly delicious.

What Is in Royal Jelly?

Generally speaking, it is exceptionally rich in natural hormones, has an abundance of vitamins A, C, E and the B-complex vitamins including thiamine, riboflavin, pyridoxine, niacin, pantothenic acid, biotin, inositol and folic acid.

135

Royal jelly has 18 amino acids, richly concentrated with cystine, lysine, arginine. It is also a good source of essential fatty acids, phosphorus compounds and acetylcholine, which transmits nerve messages and is intimately involved in brain development and memory health.

Royal jelly has an abundance of nucleic acids—DNA (deoxyribonucleic acid) and RNA (ribonucleic acid)—the genetic code which makes up life. Gelatin, one of the predecessors of collagen, is also found in jelly. Collagen is a powerful anti-aging element that helps preserve the youth of the body, particularly the skin.

Fights Infection, Boosts Immune System.

Royal jelly has a supply of gamma globulin, the important infection fighting and immune stimulating factor. Additionally, royal jelly contains decanoic acid, also needed to stimulate antibiotic activity against harmful bacteria and fungal infestations. It is this built-in antibiotic factor that helps control invasion of harmful microbes.

How Royal Jelly Is Harvested.

To collect or harvest royal jelly, the process is more involved than gathering bee pollen or propolis. Imagine trying to "milk" a nurse bee! Small wonder royal jelly can be costly. To meet the demand for this rejuvenating cell-food, beekeepers have prepared a workable method.

For royal jelly gathering on a small scale, the beekeeper merely takes the queen out of the hive. The entire colony then frantically rears those queens that the queen mother previously deposited in the larger emergency "queen cells" scattered around on ordinary brood combs. The beekeeper cuts away these cells; then he harvests the royal jelly deposited there for the tiny larvae. This method is not too efficient. The hive cannot remain without a queen for very long. Since there is no queen to lay eggs, the population will decline rapidly; honey and bee production suffer. The colony will soon die out. So this is not considered an acceptable method.

Large harvests involve mass production of queens. Basically, most commercial beekeepers routinely requeen their hives each year by purchasing young healthy commercially-reared queens. This queen-rearing process does produce a continuous harvest of royal jelly. Here is how this is done.

Larvae, Cells, Royal Jelly.

Young worker larvae, eight to 24 hours old, are plucked out of their tiny brood cells and quickly transferred into artificial queen cells, which can be made of either plastic or beeswax. These queen brood chambers are fitted into a special frame, making removal easy. Each queen cell is primed with a bit of royal jelly. Young nurse bees eagerly take up the task of feeding and caring for up to 45 occupied queen chambers. Some colonies will accept fewer cells than others.

Royal Jelly Is Made.

By the end of the third day of intensive feeding by the nurse bees, each queen cell will contain the maximum amount of royal jelly. The frames are then removed and the queen cells are cut down to about the level of the pool of royal jelly with a sharp, hot, thin-bladed knife. The unlucky larvae are quickly removed with tweezers and discarded. The tiny puddle of royal jelly on the bottom of the cells can be removed with a tiny spoon, or otherwise sucked out with a thin-nosed vacuum apparatus. Each queen chamber contains between 148 to 281 milligrams of royal jelly. To produce a pound of royal jelly, an average of 1,000 three-day old cells must be harvested in this very careful and time-consuming manner.

Preparing Royal Jelly.

The "royal milk" is immediately strained to eliminate any bits of debris. This has to be done quickly since the quality of royal jelly declines by the hour. Twenty-four hours after removal from the hive, studies show that the nutrient quality of royal jelly is sharply reduced. Freeze-drying immediately upon harvest is the only way to insure that all beneficial properties will be available in the finished product. Refrigeration storage at 35° F. is considered sufficient only if the royal jelly is to be used within one day.[36]

❖ Royal Jelly: What's in It for You?

This food from the hive has been cheered for its rejuvenating and miracle healing properties. Legends tell of Oriental potentates who regained virile powers and enjoyed remarkably long lives with a daily intake of royal jelly. The basis for this belief is that royal jelly has certain elements that extend more than life and youth and this belief is traced to the scientific fact of the queen bee's existence.

There are scientific studies that indicate the legends do have a realistic basis. Here are some reports from the medical community.

France.

Dr. A. Saenz, of the Pasteur Institute, delivered a paper entitled: "Biology, Biochemistry and the Therapeutic Effects of Royal Jelly in Human Pathology." Here are the pertinent excerpts:

> *Every day, man enlarges the therapeutic arsenal which he uses to battle against senescence (aging), the term of his life cycle and against diseases which disturb his biological equilibrium for as long as he exists. The numerous physio-chemical and pharmacodynamic constituents of royal jelly, as well as the rigorous bacteriological analysis, assure the integrity of the different elements in its composition. The use of royal jelly has spread widely and continues to be of interest more and more to the scientist, the biologist and the physician.*

Vitamins in Royal Jelly?

Dr. Saenz says that "all the hydrosoluble vitamins of the B group are found together in royal jelly. The prime role of the B vitamins is involved with cellular respiration and the metabolism of carbohydrates, lipids (fats) and proteins." He lists these vitamins and their healing powers:

- **Thiamin (B1):** Works in cases of neuritis, in the neuro-anemic syndrome. Possesses a tonic action on the central nervous system.

- **Riboflavin (B2):** Returns life to the skin, has an anti-wrinkling effect, corrects glossitis and fissured tongues, keeps body free from muscular cramps.

- **Pyridoxine (B6):** Combats cerebral sclerosis and muscular asthenia of the aged. Used successfully both orally and by injection.

- **Niacin:** Abundant in royal jelly, acts essentially as a vaso-dilator, indicated in disorders of the peripheral circulation and in vascular spasms so frequent in the brains of the aged. Its rapid action avoids oxygen depletion of the compromised region. Psychiatrists have observed its auspicious effect in senile psychoses (Alzheimer's disease) and have even administered it as a preventive measure.

- **Biotin:** This important nutrient plays an absolutely essential role in the fertilization of the ovum, in cell mitosis (cell division) and in the metabolism of lipids and carbo-hydrates.

- **Inositol:** A growth factor, a remarkable hepatic (liver) pro-tector, fights fatty degeneration of the liver, protects against cirrhosis. Considered a specific anti-arteriosclerotic agent as it favors the synthesis of phos-pholipids and reduces cholesterol, inhibiting the infil-tration of the walls of the blood vessels. With inositol, blood vessels remain supple as in youth and without atheromatous plaque. Inositol augments the esterificated fraction of blood cholesterol at the expense of the free fraction, thus reducing the tendency of cholesterol to be precipitated on the endothelium.

✦**Pantothenic Acid:** Considered by some investigators as the longevity factor, pantothenic acid is of prime importance. Acts as a catalytic factor in the utilization of nutrients, has a direct effect on the skin, hair and mucosa; increases resistance to infection. In some reported cases with animals, there was a significant increase in lifespan beyond the norm when a sufficient amount of pantothenic acid was added to the feed.

Varicose Veins:

Royal jelly offers excellent results from the clinical viewpoint, plus very significant improvements in another arterial disorder, thromboangiitis or Buerger's disease.

Deficiency Conditions:

States of malnutrition and, in general, in all states of convalescence, royal jelly benefits the patient. Simple stress, physical or mental exhaustion, so frequent in modern life, is rapidly corrected by treatment with royal jelly.

Sexual Deficiencies:

In manifestations of sexual involution, as well as in endocrine disorders, royal jelly in association with classic ther-

apies accelerates the normal re-establishment of disturbed functions by means of its action on the adrenal cortex.

Pediatrics:

Physicians have treated cases of serious underweight in nursing infants; the effect of royal jelly on weight is clearly evident; the bee food has a general tonic effect on the child. Other physicians have concluded that royal jelly should be part of the biological therapy given to children. Various clinical trials have established the effectiveness of royal jelly in serious childhood malnutrition by rapidly promoting necessary weight gain and by promoting the nutrition of the sick child, as well as in the cases of convalescent adults.

Psychiatry:

Royal jelly reportedly has a stimulating effect, mimicking that of amphetamines without the harmful side effects. It is effective for people with emotional problems and senility. Cases of anxiety, depression, shock and senility all improve with royal jelly. Several cases of long-standing insomnia have been corrected as well.

Gastroenterology:

Helps treat gastroduodenal ulcers. Its specific action is due especially to the presence of pantothenic acid, valuable in the protection of the mucosa and the healing of ulcerations.

Arthritis:

Clinical testing of royal jelly on arthritics indicated that it is most beneificial for rheumatic disorders.

Neurology:

A satisfactory remission of Parkinson's disease has been obtained by royal jelly, including a marked reduction of the trembling caused by this affliction.

Dermatology:

Royal jelly acts as a bactericide and antibiotic, while revitalizing the skin. Several specialists have employed royal jelly treatment with success in eczema, in neuro-dermatitis, and in impetigo. Its use is indicated in skin ailments with a very alkaline pH. Royal jelly has an acid pH which reestablishes the acid mantle of the skin.

We are not yet fully acquainted with all the mysteries of royal jelly, but the many therapies have been crowned with success. Physicians ought to use royal jelly above all else in diseases where a disorder of the lipoprotein metabolism exists since it activates the basal metabolism and increases cellular oxygenation up to 38 percent.

What is astonishing from the biological viewpoint is royal jelly's extreme concentration as compared to human blood plasma. The beneficial action of royal jelly is due to the presence of, and the synergy between, various substances harmoniously bound to one another and mutually reinforcing their effect.

*Royal jelly allows you to reestablish your biological bal-
ance and to confront aging with optimism and serenity. Nature has created here in the extremely complex biological
product which is royal jelly a genuine panacea for the aged
and even, to put it simply, for the adult who aspires to push
back the limits of so-called natural aging.*"[36]

Drs. J. R. Lamberti and L. G. Cornejo published a paper
called "Presence of Gamma Globulin in Injectable Royal Jelly
and Its Use in Revitalizing Processes." Gamma globulin, a protein formed in the blood, helps the body to resist infection.
Even more exciting, these scientists have documented important elements in royal jelly which slow down the aging process.
Drs. Lamberti and Cornejo have this to say about royal jelly:

*After many chemical, analytical and clinical-therapeutical
investigations of royal jelly, we can state that we have determined in its composition the presence of the globulinic amino acid
frequently called gamma globulin. We discovered this element in
the composition of royal jelly by direct observation of a series of
persons who were administered royal jelly and who subsequently
showed an increased resistance to bacteria and viruses.*

*Gamma globulin is of incalculable value to the living body.
Gamma globulin is the most important component of proteins
which participate in the fight against bacteria, viruses and toxins.*

Helps Rejuvenate Body.

In their published paper, Drs. Lamberti and Cornejo tell of
even more benefits, namely, that the protein group of royal jelly
also includes a gelatinous amino acid, which is a basic component of collagen. This sustains the mesenchyme of the reticulo-

endothelial system, whose deterioration accompanies the aging process. While humans do age via the arteries, the newer scientific knowledge says that humans also age via their collagen.

It is important to maintain and remake the collagen; it is the first importance of the body. To do this, royal jelly is important for its many vitamins, minerals, amino acids and gamma globulin.

To help delay or reverse the aging process, royal jelly appears valuable because of its gamma globulin and gelatinous collagen content, particularly when injected because direct assimilation assists blood chemical composition dramatically. In various tests, it was noted that there was a visible increase in the activity of the protective mechanisms of the body with a marked revitalization of the cells.

Drs. Lamberti and Cornejo conclude:

> The results we obtained with injectable royal jelly administered to the human body particularly in pathologic states were promising and encouraging. With the documentation of gamma globulin and the precursor of collagen among the components of royal jelly, these results become of paramount importance for medicine. The injectable royal jelly solution is a medicine which justifies thorough studies toward offering mankind a complete therapy, particularly for the aged who are too often neglected.[36]

Yugoslavia.

Drs. B. Filipic and M. Likvar of the University of Sarajevo published a paper entitled "Clinical Value of Royal Jelly and Propolis Against Viral Infections." They reported that they prefer antiviral compounds from a natural source "as they are not toxic to living cells or organisms. Should they prove ineffective they still cannot harm."

> From the natural antiviral substances, we must mention natural bee products, including royal jelly and propolis, which have a clinically pronounced antibacterial effect. From natural substances, the best known antiviral substance is interferon. It is very effective against herpes virus, influenza viruses, VSV virus and vaccinia virus.

Drs. Filipic and Likvar tell of treating various virus-infected people with complaints such as influenza, with the use of royal jelly. The doctors were able to help most of these people because royal jelly with propolis rebuilt the immune system and acted as a virus buster![36]

Canada.

A team of experts from three prestigious Canadian universities published a paper entitled: "Activity of 10-Hydroxydecanoic Acid from Royal Jelly Against Experimental Leukemia and Ascitic Tumors." Here are the important points from this paper:

> As part of a long-term study on the chemistry and biological activity of royal jelly, we have recently investigated its possible antitumor properties. We report that the admixture of royal jelly with tumor cells before inoculation completely suppresses the development of transplantable mouse leukemia and the formation of ascitic tumors in mice. Frac-

tionation studies have established this anti-tumor activity resides in the main fatty acid of royal jelly—10-hydroxyde-canoic acid.

Thirty mg of fresh whole royal jelly, or 1.5 mg of 10-hydroxydecanoic acid, per ml of cell suspension completely inhibited the development of transplantable leukemia in mice. This effect was obtained only when the active material was mixed with the cancer cells prior to administration. Attempts to demonstrate protection after tumor implantation or by separate administration of royal jelly and leukemia cells have as yet been unsuccessful.

Further studies are in progress to determine whether the active material in royal jelly causes detoxification of the tumor cells before inoculation.

This suggests that compounds in royal jelly are able to destroy tumor cells and help protect against cancer. In brief, 10-HDA, as it is called, is a compound believed to be a long chain carboxylic acid of the steroid group. It may be responsible for the queen bee's exceptional size and fertility. It has been found to have antibacterial and antibiotic compounds to help prevent cancer formation.[36]

Israel.

Dr. Ch. Kalman of Israel has published a paper entitled "Royal Jelly Effects on Faded Eyesight."

Dr. Kalman begins by cautioning:

The mechanism of the human body is very complicated. A deficiency of one part in a million percent of some nutri-

147

ent, even a lack of a tiny milligram of some component, can cause discomfort or serious illness.

A man came to me asking for royal jelly, as fresh as possible. He asked me how much he should take. I told him a tenth of a gram per day for at least three weeks. (Or 100 milligrams daily). I did not ask him why he needed it.

A week later, he came to me and shouted excitedly, "I can really see!" When I questioned him, he told me he was under the care of an ophthalmologist for vision problems. The doctor had not found any inflammation or deterioration or any detectable fault, but had told the patient, "Take royal jelly. Try it. I read in a medical journal that it can improve eyesight."

Another man came to me sometime later following a lecture I had given on the nutritional and medical benefits of bee products. He was the director of a big technical enterprise. He told me, "I can't see clearly. Everything is almost blurred. I have double vision. I am a very careful driver. Still the reason why I don't kill people in the streets is that I've been lucky."

He asked for royal jelly which I supplied. Two weeks later he came to see me and told me, "I am a new man. I can see clearly. I'm no longer afraid I will kill someone when I'm driving. I am much calmer and feel very well."

Neither of these two men are elderly. One was 35 years, the other 45 years. I believe both lacked certain vital microelements which are present in royal jelly. It is surprising that such a small amount of royal jelly restored their deficiencies and corrected their vision in such a short period of time. But man is such a complicated mechanism that a few milligrams of required material restores us to a normal condition.

For the benefit of mankind, it is my belief that it is

worthwhile scientifically investigating the effects of royal jelly on problems of eyesight under clinically controlled circumstances.[36]

Germany.

A paper published by Hans Weitgasser, M.D., entitled "Royal Jelly in Dermatological Cosmetics," states:

> *Through local application, as an ingredient in face masks, creams and lotions, royal jelly has tremendous effects at the cellular level. In regular use, the skin becomes soft and wrinkles disappear. When royal jelly is used topically as a salve on skin damaged by the effects of radium treatment, the skin heals rapidly and symptoms disappear.*
>
> *According to Dr. Elfriede Kerschbaumer, royal jelly promotes the growth of tissue in the case of under-developed breasts, stimulates the circulatory system in the case of circulation problems, works against cases of depression, and exhaustion. In the treatment of patients with abnormal hair loss or baldness, royal jelly trials produced increased hair growth.*
>
> *Ninety percent of Dr. Kerschbaumer's patients with seborrhea, dry skin, red spots, abnormally colored skin on the insides of extremities, excessive sweating, hair loss, fatigue, sagging of skin (tissue, muscles, breasts), swollen legs, digestive problems, obesity (three obese patients averaged a loss of one pound per week without diet or exercise), failing memory, lack of concentration and insomnia reacted favorably to royal jelly therapy.*
>
> *Royal jelly reduced nervousness and depression, increased the size of breast tissue (an 18-year-old woman gained two pounds growth of breast tissue in three months),*

reestablished hair growth (in six weeks with no side effects), promoted healthier circulation. All patients experienced a feeling of increased well-being.

Neurovegetative disorders in a 48-year old man, including impotence, depression, lack of concentration, blood pressure 115 over 100, did not respond to conventional treatment. Instead, three drops of royal jelly in water three times daily was tried. Results: In three weeks, symptoms reportedly were gone!

Royal jelly normalizes and increases sexual activity in both males and females; royal jelly increases androgen hormones in men, estrogen levels in women.

In another case, a 21-year old man had diffuse hair loss, accompanied by severe headaches. Treatment: Fifteen drops of royal jelly three times daily; then 2- to 15-minute treatments with a high-frequency heat lamp. In 14 days, headaches were eased; in three months, improved hair growth.

Finally, a 26-year-old woman was troubled with seborrhea on the face and head, plus under-development of breasts. She complained of sleeplessness, inability to concentrate, sweating spells, and depression. Treatment: five ampules of royal jelly daily; at the same time, ten face and breast treatments with royal jelly cream. After only one treatment, sleep came easier; after four, her concentration improved, sweats and depression disappeared. In four weeks, a four centimeter increase in breast tissue was observed. After eight weeks, all complaints were gone. Larger breasts remained."[36]

From these cases, we can see that the European scientific community is aware of the myriad benefits of this miracle food from the hive.

Before we take our leave of Europe, it is prudent to heed the statement made by H. W. Schmidt, M.D., before the German Medical Association. His topic was "Royal Jelly in Diet, Prophylaxis and Therapy":

> *The action of the active substances and nutrients contained in royal jelly takes place throughout the entire body and acts to regulate all the functions of the body. From all the investigations and observations regarding royal jelly, it is apparent this is a powerful agent composed of hormones, nutrients, enzymes and bio-catalysts which starts up and revives the functions of cells, the secretions of glands, the metabolism and blood circulation.*
>
> *To summarize, it is the interplay of all the complex factors present in royal jelly which work to preserve life and strength in the organism, which delays the aging process, and which retains for as long as possible the youthful physical freshness of the body, elasticity of the mind, and psychic buoyancy."*[36]

The United States.

Prescribed to Calm Patients.

"I recommend royal jelly to patients who are chronically fatigued," says Dr. Eugene Oliveto of Omaha, Nebraska. "After taking it for about one month, these patients usually report that they feel more energetic. "I also recommend royal jelly to patients with upset stomach since it has a calming effect on the gastrointestinal tract. I take royal jelly to relieve my allergies since it acts as an anti-inflammatory."[37]

Fountain of Youth.

Steve Choi, C.N. (certified nutritionist) also tells of the healing powers of royal jelly:

> It is reported to help in cell regeneration, inhibit the aging process, increase resistance to disease and help maintain skin tone and lustrous hair. It also is effective in treating different skin problems such as dry, scaly skin and acne.
>
> Royal jelly stimulates the adrenal glands and metabolism, giving more energy, rapid recovery from fatigue, and enhanced sexual capabilities.
>
> Royal jelly comes in a variety of preparations: mixed in honey, capsules, tablets and refrigerated fresh royal jelly.
>
> Fresh royal jelly would be the cheapest to take, but it is least practical. It is very unstable and becomes rancid easily after it comes into contact with air, light and room temperature. Also, fresh royal jelly has a sharp taste most of us don't like.
>
> From a practical standpoint, freeze-drying is the best form of preparation. Freeze-drying removes only the water from fresh royal jelly and makes it very stable, easy to carry and convenient to take.
>
> The difference in nutrient content between fresh and

152

freeze-dried royal jelly is minimal, but the advantages are great. The dosage varies depending on the case, but people who would take it seriously may use from 1000 milligrams to 2000 milligrams, two to three times daily.[38]

Conclusion

❖ The Amazing World of Bees and Their Foods

So we see that bee products do have therapeutic benefits. They offer good nutrition and health. And these foods are some of the most environmentally-safe health products available. Let's look at some amazing discoveries about bees and their foods:

• The honeybee is environmentally friendly. Bees do not pollute the environment. They do not require special land use. They are a vital part in the reproduction of plant life since over half of all plants on earth would not exist if they were not pollinated by bees and other insects.

• Bee products are user-friendly. Although hives are "robbed" of some of their bounty, this is never done at the expense of the bee, since that would be tantamount to killing the goose that lays the golden egg. Man has learned to "farm" bees for our mutual benefit. Bee products need not be tested on other animals since they are food products. In fact, bee pollen and royal jelly are used in supplements to strengthen animals. Propolis has also been used to dress wounds on pets to speed healing.

• Bee pollen approaches the goal of Nature's almost complete food. Bee pollen can sustain life. It is the bread of the bees and is the beehive's main food. Gathered from the stamen of flowers, it is a rich source of vegetable protein and amino acids, vitamins, enzymes and co-enzymes, carbohydrates and essential fatty acids—but is low in fats and calories. Nature takes care of this "food combining." All of the nutrients in bee pollen are found together in natural balance. Bee pollen is readily absorbed and assimilated by the body.

• Royal jelly is one of Nature's most concentrated foods. Where bee pollen is the "bread" of the hive, royal jelly is the pearly gelatin "milk" produced by the pharyngeal gland of nursing bees which literally creates a queen bee from a simple worker bee larva. The queen bee is maintained exclusively on royal jelly which accounts for her incredible size, fertility and longevity (she lives up to four years versus the worker bee's 40-day lifespan).

• Propolis is the hive's natural defense against microorganisms. Bees gather resin from trees to make propolis. They coat the entire hive with a varnish of propolis to immunize it against disease. Propolis contains antibacterial, antiviral and fungicidal properties which contribute to making the beehive the most sterile environment on earth. Propolis reportedly has 500 times more bioflavonoids than oranges.

The late Dr. Paavo O. Airola, outstanding naturopathic physician of Phoenix, Arizona and author of *Health Secrets*

From Europe, had this to say about the health foods from the hive:

❖ About Honey

Honey is a perfect food. It contains large amounts of vitamins, minerals, being particularly rich in vitamins B and C. It contains almost all vitamins of the B-complex, which are needed in the system for the digestion and metabolism of sugar. Honey is also rich in minerals such as calcium, phosphorus, magnesium, potassium, silicon, etc. This is specifically true of the darker varieties of honey, such as buckwheat. The vitamin C content varies considerably, depending on the source of the nectar. Some kinds may contain as much as 300 milligrams of vitamin C per 100 grams of honey.

Dr. Airola adds that the natural sugars in honey are easily digested, as they are in a pre-digested form, converted to that state by the enzymatic action of the bees' salivary glands.

Honey, notes the doctor, is an alkaline food. It contains organic acids, similar to the acids of fruits, which produce alkalinity in the system through the body's chemistry. Since the average diet tends to be too acid-forming, it is important that you eat more alkaline foods to avoid excessive acidity.

Dr. Airola says honey is helpful for these conditions:

- It increases calcium retention.
- It increases hemoglobin count; it can prevent or cure nutritional anemia; honey is also rich in iron and copper.
- In many situations, it is useful in rheumatic and arthritic conditions, especially in combination with (potassium-rich) apple cider vinegar.
- It has been used to treat problems of the liver and kidneys, disorders of the respiratory and digestive tracts, weak heart action, infectious diseases, colds, insomnia, poor circulation and bad complexion.
- When applied externally on ulcers and sores, it speeds the healing processes. "It is one of Nature's best bacteria-destroying agents. In some reports, honey-containing pollen is able to relieve hay fever and allergy."

❖ About Pollen

Dr. Airola notes, "Most researchers believe that there must be some other as yet undiscovered substances in bee pollen which must share the credit for its acknowledged prophylactic and therapeutic value. It has been demonstrated that pollen does increase the body's own immunity and also stimulates and rejuvenates glandular activity."

Furthermore, Dr. Airola has found that pollen has been able to help prostate gland disorders, hemorrhoids, promote a healthier digestive tract. It is especially useful as a general tonic, in conditions of neurasthenia, in chronic bronchitis and in treatment of the symptoms of aging.

❖ About Propolis

Dr. Airola has found that propolis is a most effective booster of the immune system and that it contains fungicidal and antiviral properties to build the body's natural defense against many threats from the environment and so-called aging.

❖ About Royal Jelly

Dr. Airola has found that royal jelly speeded up the growth of test subjects and increased their resistance to disease. "Royal jelly has an anti-bacterial and anti-virus action, particularly against streptococcus, E. coli and staphylococcus. In other reports, royal jelly accelerated the formation of bone tissue and helped heal wounds in half the time."

He added that researchers agree that royal jelly has a stimulative action upon the functioning of various organs and improves "their associative and coordinative faculties." Dr. Airola confirmed that these beehive foods "are definitely rejuvenating, age-retarding foods. They have a stimulating effect on all the vital processes of your body. The miracle foods from the bees will give you many health benefits and will keep you younger longer. After all, they have been used for these purposes for many thousands of years!"

There is a wealth of health in the beehive—you can look younger, live longer with these products made by the world's oldest living creature—the bee. The winged insect has survived some 45 million years; its healing foods may also help you survive in optimal health for a long, long time!

References

1. "Honey—Energy from the Hive," *Total Health Magazine*, October, 1991.
2. *British Journal of Surgery*, July, 1988.
3. *Prevention Magazine*, April, 1991, p. 134.
4. Vogel, Alfred, Dr., *The Nature Doctor*, Keats Publishing Inc., 1991, pp. 454-456.
5. Airola, Paavo, Dr., *How to Get Well*, Health Plus Publishers, 1974, p. 191.
6. Tyler, Varro E., Ph.D., *New Honest Herbal*, G. Stickley Co., 1987, pp. 184-185.
7. Balch, James, M.D., *Prescription for Nutritional Healing*, Avery Publishing Group, 1990, pp. 38-39.
8. Vogel, Alfred, Dr., *The Nature Doctor*, Keats Publishing Inc., 1991, pp. 458-459.
9. *Parade Magazine*, December 13, 1987, p. 9.
10. *Health Foods Business*, April, 1991, pp. 66-67.
11. Walker, Morton, Dr., *Sexual Nutrition*, Coward McCann, 1983.
12. *Health Freedom News*, October, 1990, pp. 18-19.
13. Binder, G.J., *About Pollen*, Thorsons Publishers Ltd, 1980, pp. 41-42.
14. Wade, Carlson, *Bee Pollen and Your Health*, Keats Publishing Inc., 1978, p. 94.
15. *Let's Live Magazine*, June, 1977.
16. Murat, Felix, Dr., *Bee Pollen: Miracle Food*, Murat Company, 1985, pp. 21-23.

17. Beck, Bodog, F., M.D., *Honey and Your Health*, Bantam Books, 1971, p. 111.
18. Brown, Royden, *How to Live the Millenium*, Royden Books, 1989, pp. 181-182.
19. Tyler, Varro E., Ph.D., *New Honest Herbal*, G. Stickley Co., 1987, pp. 186-187.
20. Balch, James, M.D., *Prescription for Nutritional Healing*, Avery Publishing Group, 1990, pp. 39.
21. Aagaard, K. Lund, 1974, *The Natural Product Propolis— the Way to Health*. Denmark: Mentor, p. 21.
22. Airola, Paavo, *Are You Confused?* Health Plus Publishers, 1974, p. 161.
23. Personal interview with Dr. Havsteen via transcript.
24. *American Chiropractor*, February 1979, Vol. 2, No. 2.
25. *The Bee and Human Health*, 1962, USSR.
26. *Globe*, March 24, 1980, p. 5.
27. Diamond, John, *BK—Behavioral Kinesiology*, Harper & Row, 1978.
28. Kivalkina, V.P., *Propolis: Its Antibacterial and Therapeutic Properties*, USSR: Kasan Publishing Co., 1964.
29. Balalykin, A. I., *Influence of Propolis*, USSR: Kasan Publishing Co., 1972.
30. Iojris, N.P., *Healing Properties of Honey and Bee Pollen*, USSR: Federal Publishing House for Medicine, 1954.
31. Kuzmina, K.A., *Therapy with Bee Honey*, USSR: Saratov, 1971.
32. Makarov, F.D., *Propolis Therapy, The Healing Art*, USSR: No. 4.
33. Zabelina, G. F., Thesis on propolis delivered at K. A. Rachfuss Children's Hospital, USSR.

34. Balch, James, M.D., *Prescription for Nutritional Healing*, Avery Publishing Group, 1990, p. 44.
35. Vogel, Alfred, Dr., *The Nature Doctor*, Keats Publishing Inc., 1991, pp. 456-457.
36. Brown, Royden, *How to Live the Millenium*, Royden Books, 1989, pp. 211-233.
37. "Royal Jelly: Health Through Nature," *Let's Live Magazine*, March, 1990.
38. *Health World Magazine*, Vol. 5, No. 5, September/October, 1991, pp. 19-20.